PRIVATIZATION
OF
PUBLIC ASSEMBLY FACILITY
MANAGEMENT

A HISTORY AND ANALYSIS

Privatization
of
Public Assembly Facility Management

A History and Analysis

Don Jewell

KRIEGER PUBLISHING COMPANY
MALABAR, FLORIDA
1998

Original Edition   1998

Printed and Published by
KRIEGER PUBLISHING COMPANY
KRIEGER DRIVE
MALABAR, FLORIDA 32950

Library of Congress Cataloging-in-Publication Data

Jewell, Don, 1921–
    Privatization of public assembly facility management : a history and analysis / Don Jewell. — Original ed.
        p.   cm.
    Includes bibliographical references and index.
    ISBN 1–57524–063–7 (alk. paper)
    1. Public utilities—Management.   2. Public utilities—Finance.
3. Privatization.   I. Title.
    HD2763.J48   1998
    354.72′ 8—dc21   97–43236
                                                                          CIP

10 9 8 7 6 5 4 3 2

CONTENTS

ACKNOWLEDGMENTS

Special acknowledgment is extended for information provided in the monograph *The Trend Toward Privatization of Public Assembly Facilities* by A. Marc Ackerman. The 1993 thesis was researched and presented to the faculty of the Graduate School of Cornell University "in partial fulfillment of the requirements for the Degree of Master of Professional Studies." Although Ackerman had no prior work experience in public assembly facility management, his approach to the subject was thorough and commendable.

Thanks are expressed to Dr. Don Hancock, Director of Membership and Professional Services for the International Association of Assembly Managers, for his encouragement and assistance in providing various reports and research material. The detailed information contained in the voluminous IAAM Industry Profile Study proved most helpful.

Gratitude is also due Denzil E. Skinner and representatives of the major management firms for their assistance in providing information and recollections regarding individuals and details of the development of this industry.

THE AUTHOR

Don Jewell began his career in public assembly facility management as General Manager of the Shrine Auditorium in Billings, Montana. After serving in a similar capacity at Pershing Municipal Auditorium in Lincoln, Nebraska, and the Memorial Coliseum Complex in Portland, Oregon, he became President of Facility Consultants, Inc., an internationally recognized programming and management consulting firm. He is a Certified Facilities Executive, has served as President of the International Association of Auditorium Managers, and is a recipient of that organization's Charles A. McElravy Award. In 1997, he was inducted into the Convention Liaison Council's prestigious Hall of Leaders.

In addition to numerous articles and papers presented throughout the world, Mr. Jewell authored a primary reference book, *Public Assembly Facilities: Planning and Management*, in 1978, and later a second edition, *Public Assembly Facilities*, in 1992.

INTRODUCTION

Stadiums, arenas, theaters, and similar public assembly facilities have been a part of the American scene for more than 100 years. Owned primarily by cities, counties, or states, some of these buildings appeared as features of post-Depression public works projects and an even greater number were built shortly after the end of World War II as memorials to the war dead. The largest increases came between 1970 and 1980 and to some extent during the early 1990s as municipalities and other governmental entities eagerly sought to capture lucrative convention dollars, major league sports status, or both.

Even though the majority of assembly facilities derive their primary support from local or regional sources, management practices and operational policies have always been more likely to conform with national patterns. Early studies and surveys by the International Association of Auditorium Managers revealed that in most communities once rental rates, booking and/or scheduling priorities, and staffing levels had become fairly well established, there was little change noted from year to year. Mayors, city managers, and facility managers alike were comfortable with the status quo and many may well have viewed any change as a threat to their futures.

More recently, however, increasing competition and rising costs of operation, plus growing sophistication and demands on the part of both rentors and event attendees, have encouraged reexamination of administrative practices in many cities throughout the country. For some, a change in the management plan has been, or is, seen as the solution. For others, acceptance

1

of the true potentials of the facility and adjusting management accordingly has proven to be the most appropriate and acceptable answer.

Although historically slow in acceptance of change, public assembly facility management may have passed a major milestone in the mid-1970s when a new system—or perhaps more correctly stated, a modernized version of an old one—began making inroads. Regardless of how it may be categorized, private management, in a variety of forms, is a fact of life today and must be considered a viable and practical alternative.

Because of the wide criteria and varying systems for reporting either financial or occupancy information, correct assessment regarding the management of a facility has always been difficult and inexact. Benchmarks clearly indicating "success" or "failure" have been few and ill-defined. Reference material regarding operations, marketing, administrative options, and other details has been fragmentary in nature.

Many articles have appeared in the trade press, but most of these only reflected the observations, opinions, or personal experience of individuals active in the industry. Surveys sponsored by organizations such as the International Association of Auditorium Managers (IAAM) (now the International Association of Assembly Managers) and the International Association of Convention and Visitor Bureaus (IACVB) provided great detail but all too often only served to confuse individuals lacking a working knowledge of the industry.

This publication represents both the research and opinions of others as well as personal observations and experiences of the author. Every effort has been made to set forth all known options for management and operation of public assembly facilities—theaters, arenas, stadiums, baseball parks, convention centers—along with positive and negative aspects of each system. In addition, the development of the major private management companies is reviewed, with background information regarding the services currently offered by each.

Chapter 1

IS CONTRACT MANAGEMENT THE ANSWER?

Throughout the world hundreds of millions of dollars have been, or are being, spent for the construction or expansion of public assembly facilities of every type: arenas, stadiums, convention centers, exhibition halls, and theaters. Fueled primarily by innovative public funding of one nature or another, these endeavors have been touted by their sponsors as everything from cultural necessities to economic panaceas for the ills of communities. Rosy forecasts of operational independence and even profitability have often failed to materialize, and even more disappointing is the fact that anticipated economic impacts on the community have often been negligible.

Some of the dilemma can be attributed to the simple fact that many of these buildings should not have been constructed in the first place. The overall concept may have been incorrect; there could have been a failure to identify the appropriate market niche; or the wrong site may have been selected. Troubled projects throughout the United States provide ample evidence that faulty rationale must bear a greater share of the blame than poor administrative practices.

It could be of even greater concern that vital decisions regarding administration and operation have often been neither clearcut nor finalized prior to the start of construction. Some projects have started under a generalized concept that the facility would be operated as a city department, by an independent authority, or perhaps by some type of an advisory committee. Few were presumed to offer future economic problems.

In all too many instances, after the excitement of the facility opening and the first or second year "honeymoon" period, budgetary requirements for proper operation and maintenance slowly begin to demand more and more attention. Only too soon it becomes evident that competitive factors or possibly local pressures make it impossible to maintain rates for rental rates and charges for services commensurate with the costs of providing them. There have been instances where unrealistic salaries for union workers, whether employed by the building or by those servicing same, could not be supported. Staffs of governmental employees and their customary fringe benefits have been equally burdensome in some situations.

Independent surveys through the years continue to indicate that most public assembly facilities require at least some subsidization on an annual basis. Often, in the case of theaters and concert halls, this condition had been foreseen and readily accepted as a cost of providing a desired quality of life in the community. In some cases, particularly those involving stadiums and arenas built for privately owned major league sports teams, the burden of day-to-day operation has been given to the primary tenant by means of a private management contract. Where facilities are the result of a programmed political decision to retain a major league sports presence in the community, certain maintenance or similar expenses are partially or entirely borne by the government.

With ever-tightening city, county, and state budgets, the concept of subsidization has begun to receive increasing public attention and criticism. Facility administrators look with dismay at the impossible task of reducing operating expenses without trimming services. Even when answers to the problems are apparent, implementation of changes may be impossible because of union commitments, civil service regulations, political implications, and other reasons common to the public sector.

Late in the 1970s, however, the implementation of *contract* or *private* management, a plan common in hotels, hospitals, and other businesses catering to the public, began to receive consideration from civic officials as a possible solution. Although the concept of private management for public facilities was somewhat innovative, it proved highly successful in its early applications and has exhibited steady growth since that time. Now a recognized option, the system undoubtedly represents the most dramatic change in public facility management practices in the past 75 to 100 years.

Many dedicated professional city managers reject privatization with the claim that public employees can do anything those in the private sector can do. They are correct—but only when public employees are empowered to take the same actions as private employees in efforts to economize on expenses or to seek increased revenues. Unfortunately, this is usually not the case. Often reducing costs and boosting income can only be accomplished by cutting the umbilical cord of governmental administration and entering into a "hands-off" business relationship with a qualified private management company.

Although it may be economically viable, the decision to deliver administration of a public assembly facility into the hands of a private company can result in some loss of control over the long-term goals or mission for a building. Private sector operators can usually reduce the amount of subsidization required, but often only by adoption of procedures irksome to both lessees and initial proponents of the project as well.

Surveys indicate an increasing number of governmental jurisdictions have studied and are considering the concept of contract management. Even so, privatization is *not* a panacea in itself and may not be the best solution for all facilities. The propriety of that decision should rest upon an informed and professional analysis regarding the type of venue involved and the public segment it serves.

Chapter 2

TYPES OF PUBLIC ASSEMBLY FACILITIES

The type of facility, its impact on the local economy, and, in some instances, the market it is intended to serve are major considerations in evaluating the advantages and disadvantages of private management. With few exceptions these factors will usually prove of greater significance than the amount of subsidization which may be required. As an example, if higher rental rates can be expected to result in *decreased* utilization, then the basic objectives in creating the facility could well be aborted.

In any review of management options it is important to understand the broad variety of public assembly facilities which may be grouped under any of several generic terms. Familiarity with the semantics peculiar to the industry and the events typically served by certain types of facilities is also helpful. Only then is it possible to correctly identify those venues which might be considered candidates for a change in administrative plan.

Opinions regarding terminologies vary among administrators, consultants, architects, and users, but there is general agreement on the most desirable audience capacities to be accommodated by each type of building.

Facility	Capacity
Classroom	35 to 75 persons
Experimental Theater	75 to 150 persons
Large Lecture Hall or Small Theater	150 to 300 persons
Drama Theater	300 to 750 persons

Repertory Theater, Recital Hall	750 to 1,500 persons
Commercial Theater	1,500 to 2,000 persons
Concert Hall, Multiple-use Hall	2,000 to 3,000 persons
Large Auditorium	3,000 to 6,000 persons
Arena	6,000 to 25,000 persons
Amphitheater	15,000 to 20,000 persons
Stadium	10,000 to 100,000 persons

The terms *public assembly* or *audience support* facilities are generally accepted for the broad range of buildings serving the entertainment, sports, convention, and exposition industries today. Even so, recognition of the attendant features or amenities of each type can be helpful in establishing correct identification.

Names or titles given to facilities can be deceiving. For example, the Roman Colosseum was basically an outdoor stadium even though it featured a canvas-type roof which could be pulled into place to shade the spectators. In America the term "colosseum" has been Anglicized to "coliseum" and used to identify buildings ranging from the 92,516-seat Los Angeles Coliseum that hosted the 1932 and 1984 Olympic games to the 10,000-seat Allen County War Memorial Coliseum in Fort Wayne, Indiana, that caters to minor league basketball and hockey.

At one point in time, the confusion could have been the result of sports writers attempting to romanticize a venue or marketers attempting to find a name that would best sell the building to the public. Regardless of the reason, their efforts brought forth creative entities which included "domes," "bowls," "centers," "gardens," and "palaces"—not to mention even more colorful and inventive nomenclature such as "meccas" and "omnis." This concept has now given way to corporate sponsors who pay hundreds of thousands of dollars annually for the right to emblazon a name or logo on the structure. As a result, we now have such places as the Delta Center in Salt Lake City, Utah; Target Center in Minneapolis, Minnesota; America West Arena in Phoenix, Arizona; CoreStates Center in Philadelphia, Pennsylvania; and even Tropicana Field in Tampa, Florida.

Michael Hlestand, in a *USA Today* column "The Biz—An Inside Look at Sports Business," writes, "The idea of slapping corporate names on stadiums goes back to at least 1973 when food-maker Rich Products put its name on Buffalo's stadium for $60,000 annually in a 25-year deal. Today, it's an accepted fact that sports-oriented facilities are valuable billboards, each constituting a valuable revenue stream. Regrettably, all too little of this windfall finds its way to the jurisdiction responsible for construction of the facility."

At least 32 facilities (19 arenas and 13 stadiums) that now, or soon will house major league teams have sold their names to corporations, says The Bonham Group, a Denver marketing firm. "Corporate spending," Hlestand continues, "in this name game has grown from $25.25 million to at least $753.4 million today—a total that might be higher since these generally long-term deals sometimes have escalating fees to account for inflation" (Hlestand 1995).

Apart from the confusion of what a venue may be called in its particular locality, it may prove helpful to outline some of the characteristics beyond seating capacities which place a public assembly building in a particular category.

THEATERS, PLAYHOUSES, AND CONCERT HALLS

Performing arts venues are for the most part enclosed structures designed for specific uses or special interest groups. Seating in almost all cases, other than experimental theaters, is on a sloped floor with sightlines directed to a permanent stage with a proscenium arch. Ideally, the space above the stage, known as the "fly loft," is used as a storage or standby area for different sets or scenery.

Concert halls are not normally designed with a proscenium arch, but in theaters with fly lofts which must also accommodate symphony orchestras, an acoustical "shell" is necessary to direct sound which would be lost in the space above toward the audience. The shell is customarily hoisted or "flown" and stored in the fly loft when not in use.

Theaters in the 1,200-seat or less range are rarely economically feasible, except possibly in large population centers or as an integral part of a complex of buildings. Throughout the United States and Canada, however, there are many houses offering seating capacities from around 1,200 to 2,500 persons. Some of these are better known than others and are outstanding as architectural showplaces, but most have the necessary support features to accommodate musical concerts, recitals, plays, and the type of drama or spoken word most often referred to as legitimate theater. Many so-called "Broadway" playhouses or theaters fit into this category.

It must be remembered that a theater is a specialized auditorium and emphasis must be placed on the production and/or presentation of stage shows rather than general utilization for cultural events. In brief, the focus in a theater is on good production facilities and physical rapport between audience and performer. In most cases, whether or not the facility would be self-supporting was not a high priority consideration.

Examples of noncommercial thinking on the part of architects, planners, and local arts supporters are often seen in theaters throughout the land which offer poor, if any, box office facilities, little or no area for concessions stands, and totally inadequate restroom facilities for patrons.

For the smaller venues, it could well be faulty thinking to consider placing them under the administration and/or control of a contract management company even as part of an overall "package" of government-owned facilities. Experience has shown that facilities of this nature usually serve their communities and support groups best when managed by individuals with special understanding and appreciation of the performing arts. Regional repertory theaters, collegiate theaters, and other small houses unquestionably fall into this same category.

As with theaters, concert halls are for the most part expected to enhance the cultural life of a city. Quality of the performances, acoustical properties of the house, services, and proper accommodations for patrons are without exception far more important than the cost of running the hall. Often, the availability of open dates for rental to touring attractions is limited by demands that orchestra rehearsals be conducted on the concert hall stage. Since operational expenses for these fixed-seat facilities are normally far less than for arenas and convention centers, management by the appropriate governmental authority has usually been found to produce the best results.

From a political standpoint, it would be a rare elected official who would choose to argue against the advantages of providing an appropriate place for the performing arts even if the hall fails to produce sufficient income to meet costs of operation and maintenance. The need is found throughout the world and precedents are noted throughout history where classical performing arts were the beneficiaries of financial support from royal and/or wealthy patrons.

ARENAS AND STADIUMS

Dedicated and involved user groups argue that arenas and stadiums designed for collegiate and/or professional sports are as deserving of governmental support as are theaters and concert halls. To some degree, and perhaps philosophically, they may be correct. The primary difference is that arenas and stadiums with large seating capacities offer vastly more potential than theaters for attracting both higher rental revenues and greater per capita spending for food, beverage, and novelties.

Basically, an arena is flat-floor building with fixed seating in an oval shape on two or more tiers or levels. The concrete floor area in most arenas is of a size to accommodate hockey and has appropriate chilling capabilities to permit production of an ice surface for hockey or ice shows. Except in some single-purpose university arenas, basketball is played on a portable hardwood court laid temporarily on the bare floor, or sometimes over the ice. Seating at rinkside or courtside is usually flexible in nature.

In newer venues, the club suites, private suites, luxury suites, or skyboxes, are ideally located on the main concourse or middle level, bringing the premium areas closer to the action than in the past. In addition to extensive concession outlets, most of the arenas of later design offer a wide range of food and beverage services for season ticket holders and other special guests.

A stadium is characterized by seating and sightlines designed for viewing either baseball or football. As in arenas, stadiums feature tiered seating, an array of suites and skyboxes, concessions, and a variety of food and beverage services. The once-popular concept of designing multiuse facilities for both baseball and football sports has proven unacceptable for either.

Fieldhouses, ice arenas, or gymnasiums can be divided into categories based upon several factors: seating capacity; whether the seating is permanent or retractable; whether the facility is multipurpose; geographic location; or type of ownership. A university arena or fieldhouse, for example, may offer extensive seating but its usage may prove limited due to the *type* of seating, plus the fact that both home games and practice sessions dominate the schedule.

Almost without exception, sports-oriented facilities providing seating capacities in the lower range (6,000 to 8,000 seats) are rarely of interest to major firms providing contract management. The opportunity to materially improve fiscal conditions or even show a reasonable margin of profit simply does not exist. Opportunities to expand concessions operations may be limited as well.

For large arenas such as football stadiums and baseball parks the scenario is different. Seating capacity, scope, expense of operation, debt service, interaction with business corporations, and public scrutiny demand efficient administrative practices. A number of management options can be considered with selection of the most appropriate dependent upon factors such as political considerations, the funding mechanism, or the financial strength and attitude of the primary tenant. Buildings such as these offer the best opportunities to attract revenues from rentals, advertising, concessions, private suites, novelties, and food and beverage sales. Distribution of the profit becomes another matter.

CONVENTION CENTERS/CONGRESS CENTERS

Convention centers in most North American cities typically offer one or more exhibition halls and a number of meeting rooms. The design of many also provides for a large entry lobby to accommodate delegate registration, a separate ballroom, a theater-style assembly room, a full-service kitchen, storage space, and a broad range of other amenities.

In Europe, convention centers are known as congress centers. At this time, most of the major congress centers there are lacking in dedicated exhibition space since exhibits are traditionally staged in separate trade fair buildings. There are several reasons for this difference: the lack of adequate land area in most downtown European cities in which to build an exhibit hall; the feeling of some European professional associations that the commercialism of an exhibit detracts from the dignity of the event; and the possibility that European meeting planners may not have yet recognized the substantial profits to be made by conducting their meetings and exhibitions concurrently.

An additional difference between a North American convention center and a European congress center is that many of the latter contain highly attractive fixed-seat theaters which accommodate a wide range of cultural events.

Geoffrey V. Smith, Press Bureau Chief for the Association Internationale des Palais de Congres' based in London, writes, "A congress centre to my mind is just the same as a convention centre, although in the U.S. a convention center is usually a flat floor big venue, whereas in Europe it is usually an auditorium type venue, maybe with exhibition space alongside. Exhibition Centres flourish in Europe as separate unconnected venues."

Smith continues, "The word 'conference' cuts right across all this in Europe. A centre can be a convention, congress or conference centre, almost interchangeably. We do not really have the U.S. concept of a conference center, as in the International Association of Conference Centers (IACC). The problems of nomenclature in our business are complex, and after years of discussion I can find no clear definitions. I despair of there ever being a widely accepted agreement on nomenclature, for many years to come" (Smith 1997).

CONFERENCE CENTERS/TRADE CENTERS

Conference centers differ from convention centers in that they are designed primarily for groups in the range of 75 to 124 people and usually offer guest rooms plus well-equipped meeting spaces for seminars, top-level planning sessions, and other similar activities. Most conference centers are located in suburban or "quiet" locations but with good connections to hub airports.

A trade center can best be described as a special-purpose office building oriented toward a specific group of users with a common interest in international trade. Some offer limited exhibition space for specific purposes.

Chapter 3

MANAGEMENT SYSTEMS

The importance of the management system on the overall success or failure of a public assembly facility project cannot be overstated. All too often when the time has come to research management options, little meaningful information has been available. While many of the individuals charged with the responsibility of monitoring operation of such buildings may be highly experienced in their own professions, they have little knowledge regarding the nuances of facility management. Few have ever had occasion to lease or use this type of venue for business purposes.

Bond measure proposals in some instances have dictated the creation of administrative commissions or some other predetermined management system. Even so, the proscribed procedures for such bodies do not always preclude adoption of some system other than direct operation of the facility by the commission.

Experience has proven that there must be agreement on the basic objectives or mission of a public building for any management system to succeed. Where this direction has not been present, divergent forces have continued through the years to press for their special interests, leaving behind a legacy of deficits and a trail of unfortunate managers who have become victims of the conflict.

Although many variations are in use, management systems can be said to fall into one of six basic categories. Each plan has its supporters and each offers both advantages and disadvantages depending upon local conditions, ownership, funding, and the size and nature of the facility involved.

16 Chapter 3

- Civic Department
- Branch of a Civic Department
- Advisory Board
- Convention Bureau
- Independent Authority
- Contract Management

CIVIC DEPARTMENT

A 1994 IAAM Industry Profile Study reveals that when all types of public assembly facilities are considered, the most common form of administration in North America is that where the building or complex of buildings is considered a department or branch of the city, county, state, or provincial government. In brief, a totally independent entity is created similar to fire, police, parks and recreation, or public works departments. Under this arrangement, the director or manager of the public facility or facilities most often reports directly to the city manager, mayor, county executive, or governor. In some larger cities, the facility manager may not report directly to the city manager but rather to an assistant city manager who may oversee several civic departments.

Managers or directors of facilities owned by universities or colleges often are directly responsible to the university president or chancellor. In some instances, however, management of a building primarily constructed for sports may be placed under the authority of the Director of Athletics.

The creation of a civic department to operate one or more facilities has many advantages and is, in general, appealing to most city managers. Considering the aspect of control, this form of administration is the predominate favorite of both elected and appointed officials. Special interest groups ranging from amateur hockey leagues to symphony societies understandably prefer administrative systems wherein rental rates, schedules, and use conditions are established by a council of elected officials or some city department over which they can possibly exert pressure.

In any civic endeavor the presence and use of influence factors cannot, and perhaps even should not, be ignored. Group pressures are a fact of life in the public sector and may even provide a degree of balance when weighed against strictly commercial decisions. Fundamentally, there are many who believe that when a public building has been constructed to serve specific purposes or a certain segment of the population, those citizens and taxpayers have every right to expect that the facility will be operated for their benefit and best interests, regardless of cost. The same could be said for a neighborhood park, recreation center, or similar accommodation.

In projects which have been funded through bonds guaranteed by the "full faith and credit" of the governmental jurisdiction, the tendency (and perhaps legal necessity) is for the city, county, or state to retain total control. For facilities such as concert halls and theaters, which are expected to require financial subsidization for the life of the building, it is equally difficult to rationalize any form of management other than public.

When a convention center or exhibition hall is constructed and perhaps operated with occupancy or use tax funds collected from local hotels and resorts and sometimes restaurants, it can be appreciated when representatives of the hospitality industry demand the facility offer the lowest possible rental rates and the best available dates for prospective conventions and trade shows. Even in situations where the local convention and visitor bureau may be totally or partially subsidized by one or more governmental jurisdictions, bureau officials and other industry insiders understandably believe the facility should be made available at rental rates competitive in the marketplace, again regardless of operational costs.

Another aspect to be evaluated in determining the desirability of a facility being operated as a department of a city, county, or state is that most public assembly buildings—particularly arenas and stadiums—require substantial assistance during and after many events. This help can include many necessary activities such as traffic control, fire prevention, or trade show exhibitor compliance. In short, services customarily provided by other city departments such as police, fire, etc. To divorce a venue from the city family creates the need to establish well-defined policies regarding appropriate cooperation from other city departments and to determine whether these agencies may demand fees for the services rendered.

While city managers generally prefer "hands-on" management plans, this form of thinking can unfortunately lead to the attitude that members of a facility staff are "just another bureau" and, consequently, must be treated similarly to members of the fire department, police department, or department of public works. This belief may appear logical on the surface but usually fails because a properly managed public assembly facility actually *is* different. The difference rests primarily in the fact that, almost without exception, a public facility is *rental property* created primary for lease to nongovernmental groups and individuals. Response to their requirements, regardless of the time or day of week, is mandatory if the building is to serve its basic purpose and succeed. A cavalier, bureaucratic approach cannot be successful.

The need for concerned and prompt response to both lessee and patron demands seems more logical when it is understood that management of a public assembly facility is in fact a form of property management. Although lease terms for office or retail space may normally cover long periods of time, versus the extremely short lease periods common in arenas, theaters, and convention centers, the requirements and responsibilities of administration are much the same.

Convoluted as the concept may seem, if they are to be properly service oriented, facility personnel must focus more on the needs of the lessee and event attendees than the policies of the governmental entity that pays their salaries. For example, the hours or days of a scheduled event usually fail to coincide with established working hours. Employees may not have the luxury of time to wait for the slow procedures of city purchasing to produce needed supplies.

Total quality management (TQM), the establishment of superior service virtually to the exclusion of all else, is a term which originated in the hotel industry but has been subsequently adopted by many convention center managers throughout the

U.S. in campaigns to educate employees and provide the best possible service to users and guests.

Even in arenas and stadiums catering to sports events, it cannot be forgotten that insofar as event attendees and local citizens are concerned their only human *point of contact* is usually with members of the facility staff. Day in and day out these employees confront the "moment of truth." They either do or do not create a friendly, helpful image. The single and lasting impression many visitors carry away from a city may well be the treatment received from a facility worker such as an usher, ticket taker, security guard, or custodian.

Successful operation of any public assembly facility must by its very nature be strongly "people oriented." The lessee is customarily spending major dollars to use publicly owned space and is not interested in a faceless landlord. He or she normally requires and expects at least some interaction with administration. Equally true, the event attendee may have spent a substantial sum to purchase tickets and has every reason to expect a clean seat and courteous service.

Many complaints from lessees and patrons alike are the result of poor experiences with employees. Although well-meaning in intent, the insulation and protection of city, county, or state employees through civil service has created conditions which in some instances make it almost impossible for any form of management to exert appropriate control. In some worst condition scenarios, facilities have become a virtual "dumping ground" for employees unwanted in other city departments but impossible to dismiss because of civil service tenure or protection of some other nature.

Problems for users have resulted from some circumstances where union officials have attempted to enforce unreasonable wage scales and/or conditions on visiting shows or trade show exhibitors. Because of political influence and other conditions, these forces have in some instances defied administrative corrections, leaving governmental owners with little choice but to continue the modus operandi and provide ongoing subsidies. Convention centers in at least two major U.S. cities have long been known by trade show producers as facilities where ingress/egress problems with various unions, both internally and externally, can be expected.

Another aspect which sets convention center operations apart from other types of governmental functions is the belief in some communities that extensive marketing and promotion is necessary if the center is to achieve the projected occupancy. Expensive advertising campaigns are often devised and funded; the facility manager travels extensively to attend industry trade shows and other presentations. Obviously, such practices are foreign to operation of departments of police, fire, engineering, or public works. While there may be argument regarding how funds should be spent, the fact remains that advertising and marketing budgets in some U.S. cities run well in excess of a million dollars per year.

When considering the aspect of control over public assembly facilities and their functions, mayors and city council persons may have tempting conditions which influence their attitudes toward administration. In situations where rental fees are subject to approval by elected officials, it is easy to understand when one or more of them may be reluctant to approve higher fees or use restrictions for groups predominant in their particular jurisdictions. Even on a more personal level, it is not uncommon for elected officials to expect and receive complimentary tickets for theater, sporting events, and other activities in city or county-owned venues. While such individuals must maintain an awareness of service and operational levels in buildings for which they are responsible, at the same time there are many abuses of these privileges.

BRANCH OF A CIVIC DEPARTMENT

Throughout the United States there are many cities where audience-support facilities are operated as a branch of some previously established department such as parks and recreation, public works, or something similar. In these situations the facility manager usually reports to the appropriate department head as opposed to having a direct relationship with the city manager, mayor, or city council. Of all the variations, this is undoubtedly the most ineffectual and frustrating system and the one least recommended by experienced facility executives.

Basically, operational practices for a facility under the supervision of another city department are much the same as when a separate department or bureau has been created. Such arrangements, however, do not usually accord the facility and its staff the same bureaucratic status or community identity as that of an independent department.

If it can be accepted that the requirements and user expectations demanded of public assembly facilities are different from those of the parks and recreation or some other city department, it then becomes readily apparent that subordination of audience-support buildings and their personnel to the rules and regulations of that department can present untold, and unneeded, problems. One immediate concern, for example, is that of establishing a salary scale for the manager which is both consistent with industry standards and at the same time at a noncompetitive level with his or her superior, i.e., the department head. While difficult for some to accept, it is not uncommon for managers of major arenas and/or convention centers to command higher salaries than a mayor, city councilman, or many other elected officials whose compensation may be fixed by some type of regulation or ordinance.

The concept may look efficient in an organizational chart, but an additional problem for the administrator of a public facility functioning under another city department is that of communicating with the ultimate decision makers. For example, when users register legitimate complaints about established regulations on items such as rental rates, allocation of dates, or services, this form of management is faced with the need to first convey the problem to his or her department head, who will need to present them to an assistant city manager, who in turn must take them to the city manager, who then must present them to the council or mayor. Often the matter may become misinterpreted somewhere along the way and any solution easily lost in the morass of bureaucracy.

All of the disadvantages present when a separate department is created for the management of single or multiple public assembly facilities are exacerbated when the facilities are operated as a *branch* of another department. The greatest difference is that as a branch the facility and its management are virtually voiceless and little more than a service unit of the city.

ADVISORY BOARD

Although popular at one point, the use of advisory commissions or boards to assist in administration of public assembly buildings is a plan which has failed to meet current management demands. Any benefits of the system have been found to apply primarily to the operation of theaters or performing arts facilities where determination of performance schedules, rehearsal time, and other factors are best resolved by involved citizens.

Members of advisory boards are normally appointed for specified terms by the mayor, county commission chairman, governor, or other elected official. Presumably their responsibility is to counsel with and advise facility management on matters such as rental rates, quality of services, scheduling, and so forth. It is also part of the concept that as members of the community, and perhaps even as members of the cultural groups involved, the board members will represent the electorate in directing the facility toward its best and intended purpose. Another role of a commission, which should not be overlooked, is usually that of monitoring the efficiency and conduct of the facility manager.

Almost without exception, advisory boards have functioned reasonably well during the early years of a building operation. The quality of service, however, seems to slacken when terms of the more-capable and interested citizens expire and they are replaced by others who may lack in expertise, or even may bring personal objectives to the table.

Perhaps the greatest problem faced by advisory boards is the fact that they are advisory and little more. Most boards have no voice in budgetary matters, establishment of rental rates, or selection of personnel. Few, if any, have the ability to control and/or direct management and their power is usually limited to whatever authority and respect is accorded them by the city council or other governing agency. Consequently, when city councils or other administrators repeatedly find it incumbent for political or other reasons to overrule board recommendations, it is easy to understand why it soon becomes difficult, if not impossible, to recruit the most qualified and responsible citizens for service.

In balance it must be stated that throughout the United States there are notable exceptions where elected city and county executives have respected the autonomy, independence, and value of advisory boards as buffers between themselves and the citizenry. In such cases, the system has worked well for all concerned.

In contrast to those situations where advisory boards have proven effective are conditions disclosed in a 1995 management study conducted for a midsized southwestern city (Tucson Convention Center Operational Assessment 1995). Board members reported that rental rates and performance dates in the theater were beyond their control due to the influence of symphony society members upon city council persons. Furthermore, they were powerless to reduce fiscal losses of the city-owned ice arena by increasing the fees for use of the rink because of pressure from the local university. Adding to their problems was lack of control over the hiring and firing of employees as well as certain special service contracts which had been negotiated independently by the city council. No one on the board possessed a clear understanding of what authority it had, if any.

Even more discouraging was the fact that in this instance, advisory commission members were representatives of the city council in name only; all commission appointees served at the will and pleasure of the council person who appointed them. No set criteria had ever been established for appointment. The report concluded, "To date the Advisory Commission has been ineffective. It has had unclear mandates from the City Council and it has no binding decision-making authority. The Commission's influence has been undermined by tenant and vendor contact directly with senior officials within city government. This lack of authority, oversight, and intervention limits the effectiveness of all policies, written and unwritten, and renders the Commission and the management team with little capability to run the facility" (Tucson 1995).

CONVENTION BUREAU

A hybrid system wherein operation and management of the convention center is consolidated with that of the convention and visitors bureau (CVB) has been used in Las Vegas and Reno since 1959 when the Nevada State Legislature decreed the system. St. Louis merged management of its two convention entities in 1993 and Oakland followed in 1995. Now in at least two other major U.S. cities consideration is being given to combining management of the centers and the CVB to reduce the mounting expenses of both organizations. If successful, the list is expected to grow.

Undoubtedly, a major advantage of merging the two is the savings resulting from consolidation of marketing and promotional budgets. Recognizing this fact, the San Diego Convention Center in 1996 merged its sales and marketing team with that of the San Diego Convention & Visitors Bureau even though operation of the center continued under the aegis of the San Diego Port Authority.

Hospitality industry economists have hailed the plan, pointing out that the private sector is better equipped to fill more hotel rooms and generate more business for the city. Meeting planners endorse the concept and appear in agreement that placement of the convention center under the supervision of the bureau will provide a more seamless, one-stop service and thus reduce the layers of bureaucracy through which they must wade.

This system may to some degree be limited to those cities wherein the convention and visitors bureau is either directly or indirectly funded by the city or state. It could also work in jurisdictions where occupancy or hospitality taxes are collected by the city or county and then, either wholly or partially, used to fund the activities of the bureau and/or convention center. In some instances, an occupancy tax was initially adopted to fund obligatory bonds for construction of the center itself and these costs must first be extracted before using any balance to cover operational expenses.

Negative aspects include the fact that even in cities where date priorities for conventions over local events are in effect, differences between the bureau and the facility can arise over control of space allocations. In addition, consumer show producers and locals who lease convention center facilities are understandably hostile to any plan so highly slanted toward users from outside the city.

INDEPENDENT AUTHORITY

Whether the official title be that of an authority, commission, board of directors, a not-for-profit corporation, or something similar, most independent bodies responsible for the administration of a public assembly facility have been created by some form of public ballot or governmental action. Some such bodies may consider themselves as autonomous; a few are fiscally independent; others operate subject to budget approval from elected officials. Members of these governing boards are most often appointed by the mayor, governor, or county commission chairman.

So-called independent authorities have varying degrees of authority and autonomy ranging from power to assess and collect tax revenues to the mere advising of the facility manager on policy matters. In the rare instances where governing bodies have been permitted to remain truly autonomous, some excellent results have been recorded.

In concept, much can be said in favor of an independent authority. Such bodies are presumed to be free from political influence; some may be permitted to establish employee or union labor agreements separate from other governmental departments; purchasing may be less restrictive; and operational practices may be more in common with those of the private sector. When and where permitted, strong independent authorities can prove of great value to elected officials in shielding them from the pressures of labor negotiations, establishment of rental and services rates, determination of preferential use dates, job appointments, and other difficult decisions.

Perhaps one of the best success stories can be found at the Georgia World Congress Center in Atlanta, which has established an enviable record for many years under a state-appointed authority. Strangely enough, one criterion for appointment to the Congress Center board is that the person be a Chief Executive Officer of a major company *without* ties to the convention industry. Even though new appointees obviously must undergo a learning period, in this instance it would appear that board members restrict themselves primarily to determination of policies and leave operational matters in the hands of building management.

It is rare that independent authorities are permitted to remain outside the political arena and unresponsive to the pressures of special interest groups. Since board members are usually appointed by some elected official, often such appointments carry with them implied committments. Other than in instances such as Atlanta, few criteria have been established toward determining credentials for an appointment. Safeguards to prevent selection of those with obvious conflicts of interest rarely exist.

More often than not, even though labeled an independent authority, such boards are not truly autonomous in that statutes or ordinances of one nature or another require budgets to be approved by some body of elected officials. Sufficient pressure can be exerted through fiscal control to alter the course of even the most dedicated and objective board.

While there have been no known legal challenges regarding the concept of independent boards, political theorists have observed that autonomous bodies are not truly democratic in that their members are not elected by the citizenry and therefore cannot be removed from office except by formal charges, or perhaps at the request of the appointing official. The fiscal liability of an individual board member has also been a cause for concern with some potential appointees.

Inherent to the effectiveness of any autonomous or advisory board is the ongoing problem of finding competent individuals willing to serve as members. While there is rarely any compensation, there is usually more than enough criticism, both public and personal. In an understandable attempt to avoid appointment of those with possible conflicts of interest, civic officials often create even greater problems by selecting individuals with little or no knowledge of the entertainment, sports, exhibition, or meetings industries. Regrettably, many such appointees receive insufficient, if any, indoctrination before being asked to vote on issues, often controversial.

Ideally, an independent board would be a body free from polical, business, or labor pressures. Its members would not be appointed to represent specific special interest groups but rather to assist in the creation of policy decisions which would permit administration of the facility in the most intelligent and equitable manner possible. The board would not be involved in day-to-day operations of the facility or complex but would be responsible for overseeing and evaluating the performance of its manager. Even so, such systems can succeed only when overall economic possibilities of the project are recognized and understood.

CONTRACT MANAGEMENT

Private management of assembly facilities in the United States is without question the oldest plan of all as evidenced by the Madison Square Garden Corporation, which dates back more than 100 years. Although similar in many respects, private management and contract management are not interchangeable terms. Even though most facilities in use today are publicly owned, some such as Madison Square Garden are privately owned and as such can be operated in whatever manner is deemed best by the owners. This is an example of truly *private* management.

It was not until around 1977 that the alternative form of administration now commonly called *contract* management began attracting the attention of civic leaders throughout the United States. In this regard, the word *privatization* is used to imply introduction of contract management for a publicly owned facility by a private firm which may or may not be in the business of operating similar buildings in more than one city. Depending upon a variety of conditions, systems under which the owner monitors the management contract may vary, but agreements in general establish the conditions, period of time, authority, and other details under which a private company will operate the public venue.

Private management, privatization of management, or contract management, whichever term is preferred, occurs whenever the civic owner of a public assembly facility contracts with an independent, for-profit, firm or corporation to operate the property for a given period of years. Agreements spell out the responsibilities of both parties; the conditions under which the facility is to be operated; and the basic fees, incentives, and their method of computation.

A 1994 IAAM Industry Profile Study estimated that 12 to 14% of all publicly owned assembly facilities of one type or another were operated under contract management. Civic officials in a number of additional communities were at that time examining the concept. In many of these cases, little interest could be expected from professional firms primarily due to the size of the facilities involved or perhaps their geographic location.

When deemed feasible, introduction of contract management can offer many advantages. Often these will include reduction of operation costs inasmuch as the fringe benefits of private sector workers are usually lower than those of public employees. Other benefits can be the opportunity of a private management firm to negotiate contracts with various unions; more efficient purchasing systems; relief from immediate political influences; and the advantages of corporate oversight. An additional benefit cited by private management companies is that some offer special departments designed to create events which will use the buildings under their control. With strong ties to the food and beverage industry, the expertise of the private management firms in these areas can also usually lead to increased revenues.

Contract management relieves a city, county, or other governmental entity of the responsibility of selecting a manager and monitoring his or her performance. Inasmuch as facility management is a profession where few individuals remain in a given position for long periods of time, the problem of locating a suitable replacement is one more concern that can be avoided through privatization.

On the downside, contract management in most cities means relinquishment of control by elected officials to outsiders. It means the loss of influence over which citizens will be hired, or which of them will be discharged. It means the loss of substantial control over booking policies, the type of shows to be scheduled, and preferences to be given local groups. It can also mean loss of control over rental rates and service charges. Still another reason contract management may not prove feasible for smaller facilities is the cost. Management fees vary widely but contracts calling for annual fees in amounts of $300,000 or more are not uncommon.

Chapter 4

DE FACTO PRIVATIZATION

Contract management of public assembly facilities did not initially appear in the highly professionalized form displayed today. Rather, it evolved in a gradual manner as the result of some relatively simple decisions and in response to certain basic industry needs.

In some documentations the process has been labeled "de facto privatization" and this may well be a more correct term. Regardless of terminology, the fact remains that the *concept* of partnership between the public and private sector was recognized and in practice long before the advent of overall administrative management contracts as they are known today.

In the 1930s and prior to the Franklin D. Roosevelt era of Public Works Administration (PWA) projects, most major sports facilities were privately owned and operated. Consequently, it was only when federal, state, and local governments entered the scene that the opportunity arose for management of these buildings by public employees. Management in those days was not particularly regarded as a profession since most of those involved were political appointees—some good, some not so good. Regardless of their capabilities, the majority received their jobs and departed them at the will of some elected official.

In 1924 two of the very early managers, Charles A. McElravy of Memphis, Tennessee, and Joseph G. Grieb of Milwaukee, Wisconsin, decided it might be helpful to organize a professional organization for the fledgling industry to aid in the exchange of ideas and operational information. Recognizing an increase in the number of Canadian managers, the Auditorium Managers

Association was renamed the International Association of Auditorium Managers in 1934. By 1996 IAAM membership had exceeded 2,500 throughout the world. Also in 1996, recognizing the term *auditorium* as out-of-date and seldom used, the organization voted to officially change the name to International Association of *Assembly* Managers (IAAM Historical Highlights 1997).

The post-war years of the 1950s and 1960s witnessed a flurry of construction ranging from ill-planned "veterans memorial" buildings to multipurpose facilities of every types. Owners of many professional basketball, hockey, baseball, and football teams were delighted to see arenas and stadiums provided by funds other than their own. Lease terms varied to a great degree depending upon local conditions since the lucrative income from television rights had not yet begun to make its impact on professional sports. Responsibilities for a facility manager could range anywhere from handling all operational matters to that of merely serving as the paid monitor of contract terms.

FOOD AND BEVERAGE CONCESSIONS

An early example of de facto privatization was the development of nationally oriented food and beverage organizations. Administrators in most publicly owned facilities were basically responsible for operation of concessions but possessed little, if any, practical experience. As it became more evident that greater profits could be achieved by contracting the operation to professionals able to devote their full attention to the subject, the practice of leasing concession rights soon spread from privately owned stadiums, arenas, and race tracks to public buildings.

In presenting proposals to governmental owners and agencies, concessionaires were quick to point out many of the same type of benefits used by professional management companies in their presentations today. By leasing concession rights a city or county removes itself from the cumbersome procedures of purchasing product and supplies, finding and hiring a competent manager, handling the recruitment and payroll of part-time workers, maintaining concessions equipment, consumer complaints, and liability—to name only a few. The procedure was reasonably simple. Prospective concessionaires presented credentials and made their proposals, most of which provided that a stipulated percentage of gross revenues from the sale of food, beverages and liquor would be paid in exchange for exclusive rights. Most contracts were awarded to the firm offering the highest percentages of return and were for a given period of time with escape clauses for both parties.

The extent of economic benefit to a facility as a result of leasing exclusive concessions rights to a private company has long been a subject of debate within the industry. Individuals dedicated to self-operation are quick to point out that *net* profits from independent operation should range somewhere between 15% to 20% higher than any offers that could legitimately be made by private firms. Major concessionaires counter this with the argument that because of their expertise they have the capability to increase *gross* revenues more than enough to offset the difference, regardless of what percentage is paid by them.

Based both on their experience in other markets and the fact that they are not as sensitive to criticism as would be a local, there can little doubt that outside concessionaires bring with them the opportunity to make some price increases. Still another benefit cited by national concessionaires is their ability to institute and oversee proper accounting procedures. Lastly, since the national firm is responsible for providing experienced management, it can be expected to respond rapidly if, and when, it becomes necessary to replace a concessions manager.

As the use of major convention centers by national, regional, and state associations became more prevalent, the demand heightened for dependable food and beverage service. For a time, sensing a new competitor for banquet dollars in the community, some hoteliers vigorously opposed the inclusion of production kitchens in publicly owned buildings. Even as economically sound as their objections may have been, center operators and convention bureau heads soon determined public facilities must either offer the services demanded by potential lessees or lose the business to some other city.

It was not uncommon at one point for convention center design to include kitchens primarily for finishing food preparation as opposed its total production. Some administrators attempted to appease local catering firms by offering lessees a list of "approved" caterers and then allowing these providers the privilege of bidding on luncheons or dinners. In most cases the successful caterer was expected, or required, to reimburse the center with an established percentage of his gross revenue in return for use of the kitchen and equipment. Lack of control by facility management over not only food quality but service as well soon demonstrated the fallacies of the plan and the need for an exclusive catering arrangement.

In providing the type of in-house food and beverage services required by professional meeting planners, it is commonplace for the newer centers to provide fully equipped production kitchens plus adequate concession stands, snack bars, and perhaps even food courts. In some instances, catering firms invited to make proposals are asked to indicate the amount of money they are prepared to invest for additional equipment, both fixed and movable, beyond that provided by the owner. In all cases, they are required to provide appropriate references, typical menus, and percentages of gross revenue they are willing to pay for exclusive rights. A few facilities have developed successful agreements with locally based caterers, but the greatest percentage of contracts throughout the United States by far are with national firms.

Not only have exclusive food and beverage contracts usually resulted in better service and products, they have at the same time provided a vital contribution to annual revenues for the facilities. Receipts are such that in many cases the use of convention center meeting rooms and ballrooms can be offered without a separate rental fee when booked for luncheons, dinners, or banquets.

More common in the past than now, the larger national concessions firms occasionally played an unheralded, but sometimes vital role in project development. As completion neared and it became evident that construction funds would not be adequate to purchase equipment for concession stands, kitchens, and other necessities, the financial strength of the concessionaire came into play. In exchange for his investment in equipment, payment percentages were usually adjusted downward and lease periods extended for a sufficient number of years to permit recovery of investment. In some cases a good deal was at hand for everyone concerned—except the smaller operator unable to offer the necessary startup financing.

JANITORIAL SERVICES

In addition to the leasing of concession rights, another operational contract often offered by public buildings to the private sector is that of janitorial services. In many buildings, particularly sports arenas and stadiums subject to large crowds and quick turnarounds between games or events, the problem is solved by augmenting the regular full-time crew with temporary workers provided by a service contractor. In an effort to hold the roster of public employees to a minimum, some managers have found it expedient to employ outside or private sector contractors for virtually all janitorial, custodial, setup, and maintenance services.

A classic example of dedicated effort to restrict public payroll to the lowest possible level was demonstrated at John B. Hynes Veterans Memorial Auditorium in Boston before the facility was given over to the Commonwealth of Massachusetts to become the Veterans Memorial Convention Center. Although widely used for concerts, exhibitions, and meetings of all types, when the property was owned by the City of Boston the employee roster consisted of a manager, an office secretary, and a security officer. All other workers were either temporary or employees of a subcontractor such as the show decorator, caterer, or even the leasing party itself.

A somewhat different example, and one which attempted to establish some type of middle ground, was at one time demonstrated at the Los Angeles Sports Arena and Coliseum where a minimal staff of workers was employed to provide daily janitorial and maintenance services but was augmented by part-time workers to handle cleanup and setup assistance between events.

SECURITY SERVICES

Other than employment of a night watchman to oversee the property, few facilities in the past felt a need for full-time security services. The advent of growing and perhaps less orderly crowds for sports events and popular music concerts, along with the increase in consumer shows such as home shows, auto shows, and boat shows, presented management with the need at various times to provide reasonably large forces of trained officers. In some cities it was possible to draw upon the services of off-duty police officers. In others it became more expedient for facility management and/or the lessee to contract with a private firm to provide both personnel and proper supervision. The major advantages included one statement, one check, no payroll problems, and reduced liability for claims against the security forces.

These "marriages of convenience" between the public and private sector, represented for the most part by exclusive contracts, have and do run a wide gamut depending upon factors such as the size of the facility, area population, location of the building and so on. Even though some of the arrangements have been of short duration the list has been broad, ranging from the more mundane janitorial, electrical, and telephone services to exhibit decorating.

Chapter 5

FACILITY OWNERSHIP

In contrast to earlier times when the majority of sports facilities were privately owned, virtually all public assembly buildings in the United States today are the property of some governmental entity regardless of what corporate name may be emblazoned across the facade. The entry of public ownership has been accompanied by a long list of considerations far and beyond that of simple profit and loss.

Because of this change in ownership, an understanding of the factors which have been involved in the proliferation of new construction and expansion becomes of importance in selecting the most appropriate management system. This is especially true when it is recognized that some of these projects are more the results of faulty concepts than any actual need or possible economic benefits.

As basic as it may appear, failure to establish a realistic purpose or mission for the facility has been the common complaint in many situations. With undefined goals, prospects for evaluating the success or failure of any form of management have proven next to impossible. For instance, the most acceptable management plan in one city might be one which produces a smooth, user-friendly operation regardless of cost. In another location the best system could be one capable of reducing operating costs and increasing revenues.

Although a popular alternative, contract management in all cases may not necessarily be the best resolution. After long discussions with two of the major private companies in 1996, Dallas city officials reported: "The limited financial return to the city through a private management contract does not warrant risking this economic impact" (Herrick 1996).

Illustrations of the multimillion dollar spending spree for new or expanded public assembly facilities in the 1990s are virtually endless, with the rationales ranging from an effort to improve the local economy to meeting demands of a sport team owner. As the race to build newer and larger venues continues, conservative naysayers are expressing concern that market demand may be slowing and that need for caution is at hand. They point to the overbuilding of office properties and hotels in the 1980s as prime examples of development too far in advance of demand and suggest the same could prove true in the assembly facility industry.

History verifies that the quest to satisfy civic pride has occupied the minds of civic leaders throughout the centuries as exemplified by the words of an unknown Roman who declared in 80 A.D., "While stands the Colosseum, Rome shall stand. When falls the Colosseum, Rome shall fall. And when Rome falls, the world."

There was undoubtedly little public discussion regarding feasibility of the Colosseum but the situation is different today with heated debates commonplace over who should build a facility, how it should be financed, and who should pay for its operation. Often posed, but seldom answered correctly, is the simple question, "If built, who will use it?"

Throughout the civilized world there are multiple examples—Manila, Belgrade, Acapulco, Jakarta, to name a few—where a congress center came into being virtually by executive decree. Most were the result of an invitation from the nation's leader to host a prestigious international conference of one nature or another. Following award of the bid, construction often began without benefit of adequate architectural planning. In the rush, many of the buildings were designed primarily to fit specific needs of the initial event without recognizing that meeting requirements can and do differ widely. The net result has been centers which respond poorly to market demands and are of little long-term value.

The situation is little different for sports events. For a time, professional baseball and football team owners were content to share so-called multiple use or "convertible" stadiums such as Busch Stadium in St. Louis, Missouri and Oakland-Alameda County Coliseum Complex in Oakland, California. Scheduling conflicts, field conditions, unsatisfactory seating arrangements created by the compromises, lack of private suites, inadequate restrooms, and improperly located food and beverage outlets all ultimately proved that owners using such facilities were lacking many of the profit-making features found in stadiums dedicated to baseball or football exclusively.

Throughout the United States communities continue to pursue major league sports franchise owners with promises of larger and newer facilities, plus improved amenities and low rental terms. Understandably, since there are a limited number of franchises in all the major leagues, attracting a dissatisfied owner is a quicker and easier option than waiting for an expansion team to be awarded.

Political leaders in many jurisdictions have apparently been unwilling to entrust the "build or no-build" decision to the taxpayers. In Seattle, Washington, after voters rejected additional taxes for arena or stadium construction, elected officials overrode the wishes of their constituents by redirection of tax revenues to finance stadium construction. Business travelers may protest, but those renting cars in Seattle for the foreseeable future have no option other than to contribute to the proposed stadium whether they ever see it or not.

A similar scenario unfolded in Phoenix after the Arizona state legislature enacted laws permitting county commissions to assess certain types of taxes without a vote of the public. Soon after, the Maricopa County Board of Commissioners determined that construction of a new domed baseball stadium to house the promised Arizona Diamondbacks was imperative, and appropriate sales taxes to fund the project were instituted. The political equation remains that few elected officials are willing to accept the liability of denying their communities even the possibility of retaining or attracting a major league team.

Reporting on the national trend, Charles Maher of the *Los Angeles Times* observed, "If you are going to build a major sports stadium today, you start out by digging a hole. That is where you are going to put the stadium. And that is probably where the stadium is going to put you."

Even so, there are many civic officials who take the position that if it is acceptable for taxpayers to subsidize parks, libraries, and the arts, then why not sports stadiums. As an example of such rationale, Frank Vivirito, president of the St. Louis (Missouri) Sports Commission, has been quoted as stating that *local entertainment value* was a major rationale in the decision to proceed with the Trans World Dome in that city.

To document the national situation, *Newsday* built a computer database based on financial data for 38 sports facilities built or planned during the 1990s. Concluding that "public money is increasingly being used to fuel private fortunes, examination estimated the construction boom at $8.1 billion for 21 stadiums and 17 arenas planned for the 1990s. Of that amount, taxpayers are expected to pay $4.7 billion and the total could rise much higher" (Riley 1996).

While new stadiums bring some benefits to cities, the *Newsday* study found that new venues primarily represented a bonanza for owners and players. End results indicate that while sports fans must pay higher prices for tickets and concession items, owners have experienced an explosion in team values and players are receiving the highest average salaries in history. Bidding farewell to the Oilers of the National Football League as they moved to a new stadium in Nashville, Houston Mayor Bob Lanier commented, "The paradox is that as these stadiums move further upscale, they seek to get the money from the ordinary taxpayer who's then priced out of being able to afford the luxury boxes and seats. I think it's shameful."

In balance, Mark S. Rosentraub, an Indiana University urban affairs professor and author of *Surviving Sports: What Cities and Their Taxpayers Need to Know When Making the Deal*, says, "Everyone likes to blame it on the greed of owners and players. But when cities allow themselves to be used, that's not the fault of the owners and players. That's the cities' fault" (Brady & Howlett 1996).

Regardless of fault if any, it must be recognized that the economy of sports has changed at warp speed in recent years. Free agency boosted salaries for players, and owners looked for new revenues beyond tickets and TV rights fees. They found it in state-of-the-art stadiums—cash cows with luxury boxes and club seats sold to corporations and the rich.

Some credibility may be given to the argument that construction of a stadium or sports arena in a declining downtown area offers the potential of attracting new businesses such as restaurants, bars, and similar establishments to that sector; bringing a steady flow of people into the city core; and the potential for rejuvenation of the neighborhood. The degree to which such neighborhood rehabilitation is actually pursued determines what type of environment will ultimately be created.

Insofar as arenas and stadiums are concerned, the overall problem is exacerbated when officials use public funds not only for construction of facilities but then further ensure profitability of the franchise by turning over management and/or administration of the new facility to the team owner. Some observers have likened this to that of using tax dollars to build an industrial plant, negotiating a minimal rental fee, and then turning over management of the building to the lessee.

From the standpoint of a governmentally owned arena or stadium, elected officials point out that the surrendering of facility management to its primary tenant is justified since it protects the city, county, or state from possible operational losses. In reality, such a contract more likely assures the team owner of low rent, relief from possible property taxes, and exclusive rights to concessions and parking revenues.

Restriction or outright elimination of competition to the franchise holder has been part of some developments. In Portland, Oregon, for example, management and operational responsibility for the existing Memorial Coliseum Complex was given to owners of the new Rose Garden Arena to avoid any potential conflict. In another instance, after opening of the new Delta Center in Salt Lake City, Utah, county officials ordered *demolition* of the Salt Palace arena even though the Utah Jazz basketball team had been the only lessee to voice a need for increased seating capacities.

Nullifying or totally eliminating competition, as in the case of Salt Lake City, begs the question of whether the result will be higher rental fees for nonprofessional sports events and a resultant increase in ticket prices for local citizens. Operators of traveling "family" shows such as circuses and ice shows have long complained that their overall net revenues, both from ticket sales and from concessions and novelties, have been strongly impacted by having to deal with private management in many venues.

A primary tenant with management responsibilities will recognize the necessity for a balanced program of events and understand that rental rates must be comparable to other venues if major attractions are to play their cities. Even so, with virtually complete control over dates, rental rates, and concession rights, only time will tell if abdication of administrative responsibility by public officials has truly been in the best interests of all concerned.

THE ECONOMICS

Local citizens fear Bill Bidwell, owner of the Phoenix (Arizona) Cardinals, may move his National Football League franchise elsewhere if a new multimillion dollar stadium is not provided by Maricopa County. Bidwell's posture, similar to that of other professional sports team owners, is that while a new football stadium would obviously benefit the team, it would enrich Maricopa County as well.

Arizona Republic Staff Writer Dennis Wagner responded, "Most folks never feel the Midas touch of football." He cites the conclusion of Robert A. Baade, an economics professor at Lake Forest College in Illinois, that there is "no factual basis for the conventional argument that professional sports stadiums and teams have a significant impact on a region's economic growth." He adds that Chuck Knorr, a sports historian at the University of Missouri, found professional teams bring little new money to a community because most fans live there already and would spend their dollars on something else if it were not for the games. Knorr's advice, "If you can't get a team for what you can afford . . . just do without it. If cities had the nerve to say, 'No', the price would be driven down."

Similar economic conclusions were voiced in a Heartland Policy Study entitled, "Should Governments Own Convention Centers" by Edwin S. Mills, Director of the Center for Real Estate Research at the Kellogg Graduate School of Management at Northwestern University in Evanston, Illinois. Mills believes "Convention centers should be *owned* and *operated* by private firms." He adds, "There is no more justification for government ownership of convention facilities than there is for government ownership of the myriad of other export businesses whose benefits extend beyond the local community. Popular belief and 'multiplier theories' notwithstanding, governments cannot produce unique economic benefits that are not also produced by the private sector. In fact, because governments have few incentives to manage convention centers efficiently, *private* ownership and operation of these facilities—when provided with appropriate incentatives—is much more likely to produce greater economic benefits for state and local taxpayers" (Mills 1991).

The terms "indirect benefits" and "economic impact" have become so overused and misused that their reliability has become suspect. Sharing a similar shadow are the feasibility studies which politicians and special interest groups use to support their contentions that a project should move forward. Consequently, the need to understand and properly evaluate these economic buzzwords cannot be overstated.

INDIRECT BENEFITS

Perhaps easiest to illustrate is the concept of *indirect benefits*. The average citizen can well appreciate the fact that when hundreds of delegates converge on a city, regardless of what rental fees the sponsoring association may pay for use of a convention center, delegates themselves will spend many more thousands of dollars for hotel rooms, food, entertainment, and retail purchases. Hotels, restaurants, and stores, in turn, pay out these delegate dollars for merchandise or supplies, local, state, and federal taxes, wages to local workers, and so on. Hence, the indirect benefits to a community from a single convention in terms of dollars spent have a value of hundreds of thousands more than whatever funds were received directly by the convention center for rental and services.

Illustration and identification of indirect benefits and the broadness of their impact on private business are found in the periodic surveys of delegate spending by the International Association of Convention and Visitor Bureaus (IACVB). Sixty-six U.S. and six non-U.S. cities participated in the 1993 Convention Income Study, which was conducted for IACVB by Deloitte & Touche, a nationally recognized accounting firm. Results of this survey, which included more than 500 events, were updated for the calendar year 1995 (IACVB Convention Income Survey Update 1995).

Addressing the broadest grouping which included *all* conventions, the survey reported delegate spending at $672.47 per person. At the same time, the organization or association sponsoring a convention spent $59.86 per delegate. Exhibitors at companion trade shows spent $154.61 per delegate. Of further note was the fact that delegates averaged 3.48 days in the host city.

As could be expected, delegate spending was considerably higher at international, national, and regional conventions with the per day total reaching $862.79. The stay in the host city was also longer: an average of 4.1 days. For state and local conventions, delegate expenditures were much lower but still a highly respectable total of $348.84 each. The average stay at state meetings was 2.42 days.

Defining the broadness of how convention delegates spread their dollars through a community, the IACVB survey further examined where the money was spent. This breakdown of spending generated by the event was itemized as follows: hotel rooms, hotel restaurants, other restaurants, hospitality suites, admission to shows, recreation, sporting events, sightseeing, retail stores, local transport, auto rental, gasoline, and other miscellaneous items.

An additional benefit to many communities from the convention and meetings industry are occupancy taxes. Initially, hotel and/or motel taxes were instituted to fund convention center construction and in some cases their operation. In many cases it was possible to do so without voter approval, but even with such a requirement the project was usually unopposed since residents figured travelers would pay the bill. Although such "bed taxes" may have been intended to pay for the building and operation of convention facilities, in some cities they have been mingled with city or county general funds to the point that now convention center operators and convention bureaus alike must scramble with other city departments for adequate operating funds.

THE ECONOMIC MULTIPLIER

More complicated and disputed is the *economic multiplier* concept. This theory contends that an event or convention attracts attendees from outside the community's normal sales and marketing area (SMA) bringing with them so-called "outside dollars" which otherwise would not have entered the local economy. These dollars are then presumed to circulate for a given number of times before ultimately departing for somewhere else. For example, the convention delegate pays his hotel bill to initiate the first turnover of the dollar. The hotel then pays that dollar to an employee, creating the second turnover. The employee then uses that dollar to buy groceries or pay rent, creating the third turnover. The next recipient uses the dollar for something else until such time as it is ultimately used to pay for federal taxes, merchandise, or most anything in some distant location.

Addressing the subject of economic impacts unique to arenas and stadiums in his book, *Sports, Conventions and Entertainment Facilities*, David C. Petersen writes, "Remember that the economic impact will be reduced by the amount spent by local residents attending the event who would probably spend those dollars elsewhere in the local economy if the venue at which the event was held did not exist. It must also be determined how many of these total fan dollars are spent on concessions, merchandise, parking, and tickets. How much of the total ticket expenditures at a concert will the touring act or cast and the promoter take out of the community?" (Petersen 1996).

While there may be little argument on the basic validity of the multiplier concept, there is debate regarding the correct formula to be used in defining long-term benefits to a community. For example, a multiplier of 3.5 appears to be that most used in feasibility reports, indicating that when delegate spending totals $1 million, the true benefit of that meeting to the community is $3.5 million. In truth, there may well be as many ways to prove the dollar will "turn over" 3.5 times as there are that it will flip 3.0 times, 2.5 times, or whatever.

The multiplier effect appears to attract its primary detractors when used to rationalize financing construction of an arena or stadium. Here again, there can be little doubt that almost any event will attract some outside dollars, but the questions which must be asked are from how far outside, how often, and at what cost?

Conventions are good business for any community, and this is evidenced by the millions of dollars expended annually by both the private and public sectors on advertising and promotion. Often overlooked, however, is the fact that most conventions and their attendant trade shows can be expected to demonstrate a pattern of steady growth. Sooner or later, this expansion can be expected to result in the demand for more hotel rooms and more exhibit space if the city is to retain the business. It is at this point that some decision must be reached regarding whether to build more space for a particular client or to seek alternate users whose needs can be met with the available space. Except in major markets, the prudent decision has been to look for associations and trade shows that fit the property at hand because factors other than facility size have often been of much greater importance in precipitating a move.

Addressing this coast-to-coast scramble by cities to attract and hold the biggest trade shows, Carroll Armstrong, president of the Baltimore Area Convention and Visitors Association, commented, "The bottom line is everybody's trying to get a piece of the pie. Not everyone's going to win" (Powers).

FEASIBILITY STUDIES

In defining feasibility, an unknown sage once explained, "If you want a Mercedes-Benz, and you can afford a Mercedes-

Benz, then ownership of a Mercedes-Benz is *feasible*. Conversely, although you may *want* a Mercedes-Benz, if you cannot afford a Mercedes-Benz, then the purchase is not *feasible*." Many arenas, stadiums, and convention centers would never have been constructed had that advice been followed.

An economist who has conducted feasibility studies throughout the United States once admitted that in his many years of experience he had never submitted a totally negative report. This is not intended, in any respect, to suggest dishonesty or misrepresentation. Rather, to underline that the purpose of such studies is to include all the pertinent information such as market size, competition, potential capture rate, and possibly the size of facility to accomplish stated goals. The report may also include estimated operational costs, potential revenue, and the dollar amount needed for debt retirement.

Properly performed and used, the feasibility study is an invaluable tool. All too often, however, the job has been undertaken by well-meaning but inexperienced individuals with little or no industry familiarity; factors which could severely impact market assumptions may have been overlooked. Commissioning a market study in advance of the feasibility study in some instances might well have proven more meaningful.

It would be somewhat unrealistic to believe that any economic or accounting firm would be contracted to undertake a study if the client believed in advance that the results would be negative. Almost without exception, the assignment is not to determine if a facility should be built, but how large a facility should be built. On those rare occasions when an unfavorable report has been delivered, the findings have often received little or no publicity.

Although the Mills study is primarily focused on conventions and their requirements, it must also be recognized that most producers of consumer shows such as home shows, flower and garden shows, sports shows, and boat shows are totally dependent on the availability of publicly owned exhibition halls in their particular geographic locations. These entrepreneurs battle not only with convention center management but also convention and visitor bureaus over dates on which to schedule their shows. In one city, the major consumer show producer successfully brought suit against the city for denial of the dates he believed were critical for the successful conduct of the show.

Even though repeated usage of an exhibition hall is vital to their livelihood, it is doubtful if any show producer would ever invest personal funds in a facility. Obviously it is infinitely more expedient to demand access to a hall owned and managed by a governmental jurisdiction.

Chapter 6

OCCUPANCY AND REVENUE PROJECTIONS

Overly optimistic estimates for occupancy and revenues are two of the most common causes responsible for the disappointing performances of many public assembly buildings. In reality the operational statistics posted by some of these facilities may well be the best that should have been reasonably predicted for that particular market or geographic location.

Regardless of whether private or public management prevails, experience indicates little can be done to increase the level of occupancy or revenue substantially beyond industry norms. Some fairly dramatic records for facility utilization or attendance may be achieved during the halcyon months after opening, but for the most part these anomalies do not continue for long. Exceptions can be found but the basic hypothesis is that with the exclusion of buildings constructed *primarily* for the use of a single local tenant—a symphony orchestra or a major league sports team, as disparate as the two may appear—most facility managers must seek a wide variety of events to fill a full year's calendar. Even the more fortunate venues may prove dependent to some extent upon the depth of the entertainment dollar in that particular community.

To achieve necessary occupancy a facility must offer the seating capacity, spatial accommodations, and other architectural features available in the same type of buildings in other cities; ice shows, circuses, conventions, trade shows, popular music concerts, sports events, and many other attractions are national in scope. Touring tenants move from city to city and must look for reasonably identical accommodations in each if they are to succeed in fast ingress and egress. Demographics and media support must be favorable if the event is to attract the desired attendance at the appropriate ticket price. Rental charges and service fees must be comparable with other venues unless unusual market conditions are present.

In planning certain types of audience-support structures such as theaters, arenas, stadiums, and convention centers, it is often easy for public officials and sometimes architects to think in what might be termed monumental terms, losing sight of the fact that they are constructing a building which neither they nor anyone in that particular governmental entity will ever use. Regardless of architectural grandeur or spectacular site, a facility must meet the needs of its intended users if it is to enjoy long-term success. The building must be in an appropriate demographic and geographical location; it must have the necessary support industries. Narrow interests and influences of a few must be set aside to consider what type and size a building, if any, offers the possibility of achieving reasonable occupancy and at what overall operational cost.

The profession of facility management has been reasonably compared to that of property management since, academically, its requirements and responsibilities are similar. Certain procedures common to management of a large office building, apartment house, or hotel are the same for that of a public assembly facility. In each instance, the property is leased, prepared for occupancy by the occupant, and rent is collected. The space is later cleaned and prepared for use by the next occupant. The procedure may not be a daily requirement in property management but the same basic steps are required.

What is important to recognize is that the manager or management company of a facility basically functions in the role of caretaker. Although rightfully concerned regarding the success of an event, the lessee involved, and services to be provided, the facility manager is rarely personally responsible financially or otherwise.

Sol Hurock, a great entrepreneur of years gone by and the individual responsible for introducing many touring attractions such as the Black Watch Guards and other British regimental shows to the United States, once addressed the problem of poor attendance with the statement, "If they don't want to come, you can't stop 'em."

Another prime example is that of marketing within the convention industry. There are throughout the world what must be considered "destination cities." When meetings are scheduled in locales such as San Francisco or New Orleans, for example, delegate attendance is almost always strong. Regardless of cost, the fact remains that certain cities have highly desirable images, deserved or not, and people want to go there.

At the same time it must be recognized that inordinate success has been experienced in high-intensity airline hub cities such as Chicago and Atlanta primarily due to the ease of transportation. Many delegates can leave the city following late afternoon closing sessions and still reach their homes that night, thus saving hotel expense. It logically follows that centers situated in cities in less desirable locations cannot be expected to attract as many meetings and conventions as those more fortunately situated.

Each type of public assembly facility has its own peculiar potentials and even these vary by geographic location and population densities. Conditions constantly change but usually not significantly nor permanently. Occupancy projections, "capture rate" for conventions, fiscal forecasts, and similar predictions should be entrusted only to individuals experienced in evaluation of specific proposed projects. Costly gaps between what could be perceived to be the "success" or the "failure" of a building can seldom be closed by management, regardless of its type or quality. An important question which must be asked when weighing private versus public management is whether or not there is a realistic opportunity for a private management company to achieve substantial improvement in occupancy and/or revenues, and, if so, at what cost.

Citing the need to employ differing methods of research to determine accurate estimates of future use or occupancy, David C. Petersen in his book, *Sports, Convention and Entertainment Facilities*, recalls "The Parable of the Prudent Navigator." "Printed in bold type and purple ink," Petersen writes, "a notice printed on navigational charts published by the United States Defense

Mapping Agency reads as follows: 'Warning: The prudent mariner will not rely solely on any single aid to navigation, especially floating aids.' " Petersen adds, "It is likewise advisable to caution the prudent market research analyst not to rely on any single method or research task to estimate future use. As when a physician diagnoses a patient's illness by conducting a range of examinations, tests, and inquiries, the more research techniques that are employed, the more reliable is the result, assuming that the tests are designed logically, conducted accurately, and known to be predictive" (Petersen 1996).

When interviewing candidates for a facility manager's position it is not uncommon for city officials, authority members, or others to undertake the process with little knowledge of the desired education, experience, or skills required. In all too many instances the individual who recalled the greatest number of personal experiences with known performing artists or who interspersed the conversation with appropriate show business terms was favored. Equally regrettable have been situations where the sex or race of the candidate was the most important influence on the final decision.

To their credit, the majority of private management companies currently active in the industry today present their proposals in a highly professional manner and only after extensive research regarding the property involved. Considerably more attention is devoted by these firms to attempting to understand the objectives of the owner than are usually exhibited by governmental officials themselves. Care is normally given to explicit definition of both objectives and responsibility. Even so, there remains the need for city managers or elected officials to acquire at least some knowledge of reasonable industry parameters in evaluating the goals a company claims it can accomplish. There must be an understanding of all management contract charges along with the conviction that a particular company (and its nominee manager) will at all times perform in the jurisdiction's best interests.

If it can be accepted that the *basic* responsibility for facility management is not to produce the show or event, but rather to monitor the lease therefore, prepare the facility, clean up afterwards, and then repeat the process, then the classic roles of lessee and lessor are more clearly defined.

THEATERS AND CONCERT HALLS

Factors such as geographic location, seating capacity, demographics, and whether the venue is single or multipurpose all weigh heavily in determining the long-term potential for occupancies and revenues of a theater or concert hall. If there is little necessity to aggressively promote and market the property then maintenance and monitoring of schedules for stage preparations, rehearsals, and performances may well be the important responsibilities of management.

Small theaters such as playhouses offering 400 seats or less, those located near universities primarily for academic uses, and similar venues are for the most part purpose-built structures for which management is often a part-time job or sometimes even handled by primary user groups themselves.

Concert halls, however, present more complex management problems if the scheduling and needs of a symphony orchestra, ballet company, or perhaps even one or more opera groups are to be handled equitably. The problem becomes even more acute if proper off-site rehearsal locations are not available. The problem of rehearsal times may become truly critical when a particular facility is the *only* acceptable venue for touring stage shows in that city.

Situations such as these do not suggest the need for extensive promotion or marketing of the facility. Since most of the primary lessees are nonprofit in nature and may require substantial community support beyond that of ticket purchases, management by someone both understanding and appreciative of performing arts is often more valuable to that particular venue than anyone who could be provided by a private management company. Facilities such as these usually offer little opportunity to improve profitability. Of even greater concern would be the probable criticism from special interest groups should they feel their access to the theater threatened.

For venues located in communities lacking the tightly packed schedules of organized musical or dance companies, the situation is considerably different. Here the contacts, marketing skills, and fiscal stability of regional or national entrepreneurs may strongly impact the success and local appreciation of the house. Again roles of the lessee and lessor must be respected.

In most cases when a patron attends an arena event, musical, or stage play in his home town—particularly something which may have first debuted in London, New York, or Los Angeles— he sees only the finished product. Prior to that moment, however, a broad array of individuals or groups have been involved, often for a long period of time. Some company or group of financial backers has undoubtedly underwritten salaries and expenses of the company during production and rehearsals and is now looking forward to a return on the investment. Depending upon the popularity of the show or act, its presentation cost at the local level may be stated as a flat sum or perhaps as a minimum guarantee plus a share of gate receipts, sometimes after deduction of stipulated expenses such as advertising and promotion. In some instances, a major show producer will undertake sole responsibility for scheduling a tour and its promotion. In other situations, the producing company may sublet, so to speak, portions of the tour to regional promoters more familiar with facilities and promotional eccentricities of their particular sections of the country.

Regardless of who it may be, someone in the role of "promoter" must undertake responsibility, operationally and fiscally, for leasing the theater, arranging for ticket sales, securing local musicians and stagehands, scheduling advertising and promotion, and a score of other vital tasks to ensure the success of the engagement. If the run is well received and many tickets sold, this promoter should make a profit. If not, this promoter will lose money. Needless to say, because of the risk factor in most presentations, whether concerts by popular music artists or stage shows, whoever underwrites the venture must be convinced that a community will appreciate and support the attraction.

Some attractions enjoy such popularity that there is little, if any, risk factor. There is, however, always the possibility of a downside of one nature or another: the featured performer becomes ill; unexpected weather besets the area; a national or regional tragedy occurs. The basic fact is that the promotion of events is a gamble much like other business ventures. One can make or one can lose money. Often when the latter occurs more than the former, a city may find its theater being bypassed by promoters who have become convinced the area will not support certain types of shows or attractions. The obvious end result is too many dark nights.

To alleviate some of the risk factor for promoters or other potential theater lessees, some venues permit co-promotion wherein the governmental jurisdiction which owns the facility to a degree shares the risk with the promoter. In most cases liability on the part of the facility owner is usually limited to the rent. In other words, the house receives a stipulated percentage of gate receipts but no guarantee of a specific minimal dollar amount. While such a policy could perhaps encourage use of the facility for some marginal shows or events with no dependable or proven success record, it does present the ethical, and possibly legal, question of whether such a venture, offering the possibility of receiving less than the authorized rental fee, is the appropriate action for a governmentally owned property. Even more importantly, upon whose decision and under what circumstances should the risk be undertaken.

To circumvent the possibility of legal liability, there have been cities where local industries and business leaders have created independent funds which theater managers could use as guarantees for shows which independent promoters believed could prove money-losers. Because private funding is involved, definitive reports on the financial results of such ventures are not available. Suffice it to say, there is little evidence to support any industry trends toward so-called self-promotion. Industry veterans are quick to observe that if a professional promoter has determined that a particular show could offer a strong loss potential, why then would the opinion of an another individual, an amateur so to speak, (and in this case, a venue manager who faces no personal risk other than that of the possible loss of ego) be more correct?

ARENAS AND STADIUMS

Many of the same basic management responsibilities, or perhaps concepts, appropriate in theaters and concert halls can be applied to mid-to-small arenas, multi-purpose buildings, or stadiums. For the most part facilities of this size and nature are located in communities with small or moderate populations or possibly on university or college campuses. In such situations, management alternatives are usually limited. Contract management, at least at this point in time, is rarely an option.

If the term *midsize* can mean an arena offering 10,000 to 12,000 seats or less, it can be assumed that a fundamental part of the annual events calendar will be comprised of minor league hockey or basketball, high school or college basketball, popular music concerts, and family entertainment such as ice shows and circuses. In virtually every case, a team, promoter, or similar rentor is the short-term lessee of the building, assumes financial risk for the activity, presents the event, and moves on. The operational role of facility management has been to prepare the arena for the lessee's event, monitor use of the property, collect the rent, and clean the house for the next lessee.

Insofar as potential arena lessees are concerned, it is important to note that while many single performers, concerts, country-western shows, and touring events may be underwritten and booked by promoters, representatives of major attractions such as a circus or an ice show usually prefer to deal directly with facility management. A local or regional promoter is of little benefit to an organization such as Ringling Bros.-Barnum & Bailey Circus, whose full-time staff includes tour directors, advance publicists, and everyone else needed to insure the success of an engagement.

Private management companies are quick to point out that one of their strengths is the relationships of their employees with the agencies and/or promoters responsible for routing and booking the national tours of recording artists, family shows, and other events. By developing "package" deals wherein the attraction will play several of the arenas controlled by a particular company, private operators contend they can often influence attractions to include on the tour some of the less important or possibly smaller properties which might otherwise be bypassed. This in itself could be a major advantage for a national firm over any public employee whose negotiating authority is limited to a single facility.

Knowledge of how the industry works, the identity of the principal players, and the idiosyncrasies of the local market are indeed advantageous. The point which must be recognized, however, is that regardless of the management system employed—public or private—attractions must enjoy sufficient ticket buyer response to ensure their return to a city year after year. It is difficult for any type of administration to improve occupancy when the local market lacks fiscal vitality. Rarely has management in any so-called midsize arena demonstrated any conclusive proof that it can viably serve both as lessee and lessor on a long-term basis.

With few exceptions across North America, smaller stadiums or baseball parks are single-purpose in nature. Scheduling opportunities are limited in a great degree to a single team, whether it be college, university, or minor league in nature. As in the case of small to midsize arenas, most of these venues are managed by the primary user. The opportunity to significantly impact either occupancy or revenues is minimal.

In considering smaller facilities, there is apparently sufficient demand for qualified individuals to operate sports-oriented buildings such as ice arenas that the University of Michigan's Sports Facilities Research Laboratory has developed a Facility Management Program. Under this plan students can obtain a master's degree in facility management and at the same time acquire academic and professional experience in sport, recreation, and club management. The director of the program boasts a 100% job placement rate, with graduates currently managing facilities throughout the United States.

For managers of arenas serving as homes for major league basketball and hockey teams throughout North America, development of sufficiently flexible schedules to provide the most desirable dates for their National Basketball Association and National Hockey League games is a primary responsibility. From that point, the rest of the calendar is usually filled by a wide variety of annual events and attractions. It must be remembered, however, that the majority of these buildings are located in major markets and that most of the major touring shows are seeking dates there. Aggressive marketing of a busy property is fortunately not the No. 1 priority for management.

Whereas most of the major arenas in America once were privately owned and operated, professional team owners today enjoy such strong support from their fans and local officials that even though the majority of arenas housing major league hockey and basketball teams are *publicly owned*, they are *privately managed* by their major tenants. Few businesses in North America could hope to improve on that scenario.

Similar in nature to arena responsibilities, management of stadiums has, nevertheless, become more sophisticated and specialized in recent years as the trend toward single-purpose facilities has grown. Whereas multipurpose facilities such as the Astrodome in Houston, Superdome in New Orleans, Kingdome in Seattle, and Busch Stadium in St. Louis were once considered highly acceptable for both professional football and baseball, recent years have seen owners demanding that single-purpose stadiums be constructed to ensure the team's continued presence in the community.

Much has been written and argued regarding the propriety of building multimillion dollar properties for private use, but the fact remains that major league football and baseball team owners have assumed the position that "appropriate" facilities must be provided if they are to survive in the highly competitive professional sports marketplace. As with arenas, stadiums and ballparks dedicated to the primary use of one team are normally leased in one manner or another to the resident professional club and subsequently managed by that lessee.

Experience has proven throughout the industry that there is little logic for the intrusion of public management in arenas dominated by professional sports ownerships. Rather, local governments have seen fit to negotiate contracts with their major tenant, requiring payment of whatever rents may be needed to meet bonded indebtness and long-term maintenance of the property, but often yielding some rights to revenues such as rent from other tenants, luxury suites, concessions, novelties, food and beverage, and other sources. In these situations, team owners have for the most part opted to organize and employ their own management team as opposed to seeking the services of an outside firm.

CONVENTION CENTERS AND EXPOSITION HALLS

A convention center in almost any city of reasonable size and geographic location can usually achieve many benefits from an alliance with a private management company. Such possibilities, of course, assume that civic administration has failed to demonstrate the competency needed to achieve anticipated goals. Even though the private operator may have little chance to improve occupancy, opportunities are often at hand to reduce operational costs and often increase non-rental revenues as well.

The growing number of convention centers and congress centers throughout North America and other parts of the world indicates "product" (meaning the venues) is far in excess of demand, at least for the present time. Whether economic conditions and other factors will change the outlook is yet to be seen. What has been visibly demonstrated in the past several years is that "the big ones get bigger" and the others scramble as best they can. One has only to note the increase in million-plus square foot exhibition halls in Chicago, Las Vegas, Atlanta, and elsewhere to verify this conclusion.

For many easy to understand reasons, convention centers located in cities able to meet the requirements of meeting planners have performed well. In every case, however, these cities have excellent airline schedules, ample first-class hotel rooms located near the center, adequate meeting rooms and exhibition space, and are situated near population densities.

Conversely, in those cities where convention facilities have been constructed primarily at the insistence of private interests or perhaps just to "keep pace" with some other city, results have been poor. When the most basic requirements such as adequate hotel rooms, transportation, and convention center square footages cannot be provided, the chances of attracting national, regional, or state associations or groups are slim indeed. There may well be a market niche for almost any size building in any city, but to find and serve that narrow target is a task unto itself.

Even with the most successful center it must be understood that true "occupancy" or use days may be limited to some figure in the range of 72 to 75 percent. Unfortunately, there are no standard, industry-wide rules with regard to determining occupancy of a center. For example, some managers report a building as "occupied" if but a single meeting room is used; some use the term for the days used for ingress or egress of a trade show. Regardless, it is virtually impossible to achieve anything resembling 100% occupancy simply because of national and religious holidays when groups hesitate to meet, the cyclical nature of convention schedules, time required for move-in and move-out (ingress and egress), short lapses of time between meetings, and other unavoidable conditions. The need to understand and recognize reasonable occupancy goals cannot be overstated in evaluating competency of management, whether private or public.

Whether or not the management of a publicly owned convention center should, or can, substantially impact the marketing of the facility for either association or corporate meetings has been a subject of heated debate for many years. Local convention bureau officials reasonably contend that as the collective representative of a city, solicitation of conventions should be their responsibility. Not infrequently, management of a convention center may feel the sales efforts of the bureau are ineffective, or perhaps that attention is slanted toward tourism, making it necessary for the center staff to undertake and finance a separate, specific advertising and promotional campaign. Regardless of the rationale, hundreds of thousands of dollars are spent annually by the management of some convention centers to extoll the virtues of their facility to prospective users. Regrettably, more often than not, there is little or no system of periodic reviews to evaluate the effectiveness of such programs.

Continued shifts in top-level management of Convention and Visitor Bureaus throughout the country could conceivably give substance to charges that some bureaus do not perform to local expectations. Further, there can be little doubt that some bureau leaders may be more oriented to overall tourism and visitor demands and those of major hotel or resort properties than to conventions. Even so, a more economical solution to the problem would seem to be correction, improvement, or redirection of a bureau's objectives as opposed to the center staff attempting to market what is recognized as only one part of the total convention "package."

Certain components must be present if the city is to be considered a viable convention site. Granted, the convention center must offer adequate exhibit space and a sufficient number of meeting rooms, but of equal importance is the availability of the necessary number of first-class hotel rooms, preferably within easy walking distance of the center. Along with this must be availability of transportation, both nationally and locally, for delegates plus good retail shopping, restaurants, entertainment, post-convention tours, and other amenities.

Even when all local conditions are favorable, those involved in convention sales are still confronted by the fact that most associations move their meetings geographically across the United States, often by time zones, on a yearly basis. In situations where two or more cities are competing for a convention which regularly moves across the U.S., the selection of either one usually means the other will have no opportunity to even extend an invitation for the next three or four years.

Some groups are "weather oriented" in that they only consider sites located where good climatic conditions can be expected at the time of their meeting. Still others attempt to schedule meetings as much as possible in heavily populated areas where their membership is largest.

Convention center marketing personnel face still another problem common to the industry in that only a small portion of all associations or corporations require meeting rooms and other space in excess of that offered by many large hotels. Almost without exception meeting planners find it advantageous to keep their conventions in hotels as long as possible. Only when the demand for meeting rooms, plenary sessions, and exhibition space exceed those found in hotels do most planners begin to seriously consider public venues.

Even though an aggressive convention center representative may successfully market his property to a convention, it still remains the responsibility of the bureau to obtain the necessary hotel room commitments, contact other venues which may be required for some special session, make necessary arrangements with the host committee, and generally coordinate all aspects of the convention to the satisfaction of the meeting planner. Only then can leaders of an association move forward to consider a proposal.

Without attempting to resolve the long-standing argument regarding who should do what, it should be observed that in some of the nation's most successful convention cities the bureau and its staff carries the brunt of the sales and promotion burden. In all such cases, there is close cooperation and coordination between the center and the bureau. Center management stands prepared to assist bureau personnel by participating in sales contacts, assisting in exhibits at industry events, and by other means, but the bureau carries the basic marketing responsibility.

In many cities across the United States, an additional handicap toward improving overall convention center occupancy figures is that local regulations provide protection or "priority dates" for conventions. The logic follows that since the center was perhaps constructed, or is maintained by, funds from a hotel occupancy tax, *no dates for events other than conventions* can be confirmed by center management until a proscribed number of months in advance . . . sometimes as few as 12 but more often around 15 months.

Promoters and producers of consumer shows such as home shows, auto shows, flower and garden shows, sports shows, and many others decry the priority concept. Some have successfully brought legal action to continue, or acquire, what they believe to be the most appropriate dates for their events. Here again, the value of close communication and understanding between center and bureau management cannot be overestimated. Consumer shows are of extreme value not only to the financial success of a convention center but to many retail outlets in the city. Many also provide low-cost family entertainment to the community. In most cases knowledgeable management, either private or public, along with careful long-term scheduling can usually enable the two forces to share a common facility successfully.

Chapter 7

OPERATIONAL PROPOSALS

In evaluating the advantages or disadvantages of private management for any public assembly facility, it is incumbent that civic officials responsible for making the decision understand all options that may be available. While an existing situation may be less than desirable, evidence should overwhelmingly confirm that outsourcing of management responsibilities to a private firm has the potential to solve at least most of the problems, that the results will balance the costs, and that the concept will be acceptable in the community.

Far too often, officials in one city observe the success of privatization in another community and improperly assume that a similar move would be the answer for their situation. Steps toward such a drastic change in the management process, if undertaken hastily and without proper study, can prove unnecessarily disturbing to current employees and, even worse, embarrassing should little or no interest be shown by private management companies.

Assuming dissatisfaction with management, staff attitude or performance, fiscal results, or other aspects of operation, several alternate procedures may be considered. One option would be to employ the services of an experienced operational or economic consultant to verify if improvements are indeed possible and that a change in management style would be the appropriate move. For new projects, reexamination of earlier forecasts of occupancy and revenues to determine their accuracy is highly recommended. Often in well-meaning efforts to boost project viability, overly optimistic forecasts of probable business have been made only to fade in the reality of location or competition.

Another procedure would be informal discussions with representatives of private management firms to seek their views regarding operational procedures in existing properties or, if more appropriate, their concepts for serving the needs of a new facility. While contacts with possible bidders on governmental contracts must be handled openly and with extreme discretion to avoid any hint of favoritism or collusion, such discussions should prove not only educational but beneficial as well to all concerned. Fact-finding meetings could also provide a degree of assurance to public officials that if formal requests for proposals are issued, a reasonable number of qualified bidders will respond.

All of the major private management companies employ marketing representatives whose primary objective is to identify and familiarize themselves with existing or proposed facilities on which they might someday be invited to submit proposals. Not infrequently, governmental authorities are surprised to learn that the private operators are already well aware of their local situations. Even though the opinions and recommendations of a private management firm may be understandably self-serving, it is also important to recognize that no major operator would be interested in spending the time or money required to bid for operation of a venue which might prove an embarrassment to the company.

REQUEST FOR QUALIFICATIONS (RFQ)

Preliminary to development of a Request for Proposals (RFP) for management services, issuance of a Request for Qualifications (RFQ) is highly recommended. The RFQ has many advantages for both parties. Initially, it defines the extent of the services to be provided and serves as a procedure through which interested firms and their qualifications can be verified. For the prospective bidder, the RFQ provides an opportunity to become more familiar with the project prior to the commitment of a firm proposal.

An additional value of the RFQ insofar as governmental

officials are concerned is that it can serve as a screening device to eliminate or discourage bidders lacking the credentials or capabilities to provide the required services. Situations are not uncommon where local individuals or firms with little or no experience have attempted to become involved. Without the screening provided by a RFQ, issuance of a RFP could easily result in the possible receipt of a highly attractive offer but one fraught with impossible projections. Legislation in many jurisdictions is such that it is difficult to justify rejection of the low or "best" bid in favor of one more realistic but of seemingly lesser monetary value.

Through use of the RFQ interested bidders are invited to acquaint themselves with the property or planned project and to provide company histories, biographical information on principal officers, profiles of facilities currently managed, and client references. Through this process marginal or less qualified firms can be identified, thus reducing the field of prospective bidders only to those whom the owner is confident can perform as required. Many of the same elements contained in a Request for Proposal can, and are, used in the Request for Qualifications. The primary difference is that the RFQ does not seek information regarding fees, incentives, or performance goals from the bidder.

Inherent to successful use of both the Request for Qualifications and the Request for Proposals is the need to ascertain that announcements or advertisements are received by all prospective bidders. While it can be expected that the nationally oriented management firms will be well informed regarding major properties and the possible interest in their privatization, it may prove necessary for smaller venues to expend extra effort to publicize their needs. Potential sources of information in locating providers of services required are trade publications and referrals from organizations such as the International Association of Assembly Managers or the Urban Land Institute.

REQUESTS FOR PROPOSALS

Although Requests for Proposals (RFP) have no specific requirements or restrictions, there are many commonalities among them. There appears to be no limit to the length of an RFP (some exceed 100 pages); neither is there a ceiling to the amount of information which can be included. There are, however, several components which appear common in virtually all such requests. Seemingly each new writer of an RFP must review documents from other venues and then select the portions he or she considers most appropriate for the project at hand.

It is necessary for an RFP to provide extensive and detailed information regarding the facility or facilities for which management services are sought, the community in which it is located, specific operational responsibilities which must be addressed, plus all prior agreements or commitments which may be in effect. For ongoing properties, the RFP should set forth all possible historical data relating to occupancy, attendance, events presented, financial pro formas, personnel information, labor commitments or agreements, long-term contracts, and other matters. Of even greater importance should be a clearly defined mission statement for the facility as well as specific objectives in seeking a private operator.

PROPOSAL RESPONSES

Responses to Requests for Proposals present both challenges and opportunities for private management companies. A written proposal demands the bidder not only establish credibility, but propose strategies and action plans as well. The introductory section of most proposals will include a company history, detail experience in the industry, and list all relevant current contracts and/or clients.

Other information common to most proposals:

- A statement regarding the merits of private versus public management.
- Biographical information on principal officers, corporate support personnel, and their professional expertise.
- Identification of each facility currently managed, including information regarding major events handled.
- Client references and professional affiliations.

- An outline of the proposed on-site management structure.
- An in-depth definition of specific management services to be provided.
- A proposal for the base management fee and incentive structure, plus the method of determining same.
- Where appropriate, identification of the individual to whom the bidder proposes to assign on-site management responsibilities if selected.

Assuming the Request for Qualification process has reduced the field to only those firms that appear capable of providing the desired services, a primary feature which can differentiate one response from another is the inclusion of specific recommendations. Outlining strategies to improve or resolve problems in a facility, whether operational or political, can do much to illustrate not only the preliminary investigation a bidder has conducted but also his or her ability to provide a solution.

Practices for selection of the successful bidder vary, but the most common is for finalists to make in-person presentations to the selection committee or board. Usually firms are then ranked with the understanding that the one whose proposal is considered the best will be awarded the contract, assuming that mutually agreeable terms can be negotiated. If not, discussions will then be undertaken with the second-ranked company.

Once proposals have been rated it is not uncommon for review boards to schedule additional and separate interviews with the individual the favored firm has chosen to serve as general manager or director of the venue in question. It is easy to envision situations where the selection committee likes all aspects of a particular proposal but perceives the designated manager to be unacceptable for that particular community. The importance of trust and a good relationship between governmental officials and the facility manager cannot be overstated.

Chapter 8

SPECIALIZED SERVICES

A decision to seek the services of a private company may not necessarily indicate the intent of a governmental agency to enter into an all-encompassing management agreement. Still, initiation of a working arrangement in one area of basic services can prove to be a starting point in that direction. Possibilities are wide-ranging and in some instances have intruded upon professional services traditionally provided by economists, accountants, planning consultants, and others.

Whether private management firms should presume to offer specific services that might be considered outside their accepted areas of expertise is a matter of debate within the industry. Professionals with credentials in a given field are quick to point out that their work is more objective and that only they can offer the benefits of long-term experience. If private firms do not offer certain special services, their competitors may, thus putting them at a marked disadvantage. Unfortunately, decisions to award certain contracts are often made by those unfamiliar with the expertise required for proper performance of the tasks at hand.

In lieu of a long-term, broad-based management contract, some of the more common professional services which are offered by private firms include:

- Consulting Services
- Personnel Recruitment
- Pre-opening Services
- Event Production and Promotion
- Food and Beverage

- Custodial and Maintenance Services
- Promotion and Marketing

CONSULTING SERVICES

While communication between public officials and private management company representatives can prove highly beneficial, the situation becomes somewhat different when consulting services are involved. Understandably, a private operator may be willing to offer planning and pre-opening assistance at highly discounted rates both to become familiar with the project and to develop a relationship with the client. For good or ill, the potential is created for self-serving findings and recommendations.

A primary requirement for governmental representatives should be retention of the best possible professional assistance whether it be economic, architectural, or in other fields of expertise. Even though most management firms are of high repute and may operate a variety of public assembly facilities, this does not necessarily guarantee that their employees have the training or experience to properly undertake feasibility studies, to conduct market studies, or to develop reliable economic pro formas. The same comment applies to development of programmatic or spatial recommendations and other details involved in pre-architectural programming.

It should not be assumed that simply because someone is employed by a private management organization he or she is automatically qualified in all aspects of the planning, operation, management, and equipping of every type of facility. While employees may possess skills highly useful to their companies in certain areas of endeavor, many of them have never been involved in any aspect of hands-on facility management. Few are certified public accountants, economic experts, certified facility executives, or architects.

Whether seeking someone to perform a feasibility and/or marketing study, develop a functional program of spaces for use by the designing architect, or advise on food and beverage matters, it is imperative for the owner to know the specific individual or individuals who will be providing the services as well as their qualifications. In short, companies may be highly responsible and have enviable reputations, but companies as such don't perform the work—people do.

PERSONNEL RECRUITMENT

The mere fact that a private management company is willing to undertake responsibility for providing competent management and operational personnel is in itself of considerable value. Unfortunately, while it has never been difficult to find men and women interested in top-level facility management positions, there has long been a shortage of truly qualified and dedicated persons.

One of the major reasons for the lack of suitable candidates is that, unlike the hotel industry, there are few specific educational opportunities available for those interested in pursuing facility management careers. The most common recommendation to date has been for an individual to acquire a business administration degree and then seek employment in the industry to acquire hands-on experience.

Only a few universities in the United States offer graduate study in facility management. Where available, most courses are, or have been, taught by active managers on a part-time basis. While the University of Michigan currently features a "facility management program," examination of the curriculum indicates the subjects offered focus primarily on the operation of ice arenas. The International Association of Assembly Managers (IAAM) offers a short-term school annually at Oglebay Park in Wheeling, West Virginia.

Another reason for the lack of educational opportunities may be that there are so few executive positions available in the industry. No truly accurate method is available by which to determine the number of top jobs in North America, but some estimates can be made from data collected in the Industry Profile Study (IPS) conducted by the IAAM in 1994. This survey indicated a total of 453 facilities of *all* types, ranging from the smallest theater to the largest stadium. However, since all facility managers are not necessarily members of the IAAM and that information on some buildings was not provided, a reasonable assumption can be made that the totals might represent only 80% of the so-called facility universe. Using this rationale it becomes possible to estimate a grand total of 540 public assembly facilities in the United States and Canada. Of this number, fewer than 50%, or only 270 venues in all of North America, would appear to present truly long-term career opportunities.

The majority of individuals holding top-level executive positions today entered the industry with credentials ranging from law to accounting to sports management. Some were civil service employees assigned to a facility operating as a department of a city. Most, however, can attribute their entry into facility management to the simple fact that someone or some board was impressed by them and thought they could do the job.

Of equal concern to young men and women considering facility management as a career is the fact that in all but the largest communities there is only one such position in a city. The opportunity to change jobs or improve working conditions without transferring to another locality is present in many professions, but is rarely found in facility management. Consequently, when an individual resigns or is discharged from a particular building it usually means moving if he or she wishes to remain in the industry.

Historically, the career path of many long-time IAAM veterans has included a beginning position in a small facility, advancement to a building of mid-size, and finally the move to a "major operation." While some of the current general managers or directors may have started their careers in low-level entry positions and progressed to management of the same facility, smaller facilities to a great extent have been, and probably still are, the primary training sites for the industry.

Other than by reviewing verified experience records and references, it is often difficult to identify qualified management candidates. One response to the problem has been the Certified Facility Executive (CFE) program established and operated by the IAAM. Under this plan, interested managers are credited for academic achievements, job experience, participation in IAAM educational programs, association leadership, and other activities. After meeting established criteria, candidates must then successfully pass oral examinations by a certification board to receive the accreditation. Even though the CFE program is in its second decade, many governmental officials are still unaware of its existence and unfamiliar with the level of expertise and professionalism it represents.

While many major hotel management organizations such as Hyatt, Ritz-Carlton, and others have highly organized and effective management training programs for their new hires, the concept is virtually unknown in the public sector where employees to a great extent have been engaged to perform a specific task. Intern programs wherein aspiring facility managers could work a short time in the department of one facility and then transfer to another building in another city to acquire experience in a different division have been attempted without much long-term success.

Recognizing this, some of the private management companies are making commendable strides in developing programs which their officials hope will prepare men and women for advancement into executive positions when needed. The probability of success for the program is high. For example, in instances where a particular candidate for a general manager's post might not be readily acceptable to the owner because of age or lack of experience, the fact that the private management company stands ready to support the nominee manager with all necessary resources from its more experienced corporate staff tends to alleviate whatever concerns might exist. This concept may well have strong appeal to some of the better candidates seeking an opportunity to enter the profession.

Although some individuals or groups may seek the political advantages to be gained by controlling the appointment of a director or general manager, there can then be little doubt that the chances of securing a qualified manager are higher by working with a private management company than through procurement agencies, headhunters, or any other system. If an error in judgment occurs by either party, replacement is usually achieved rapidly and with a minimum of publicity.

PRE-OPENING SERVICES

Shifting of administrative responsibility for an established facility from public to private management usually requires acceptance of many existing contracts and agreements, with changes to be made as opportunities arise. The situation, however, may be more complex in the case of communities with buildings under construction that are to be managed by a private company.

If, for example, adequate funds have not been budgeted for pre-opening expenses and activities, counseling with the owners on the necessity of finding and allocating necessary dollars is usually an early task. Understandably, agreements must be reached on this subject prior to the start of any management service, but regardless of whether management is public or private, the development of contract documents, lease terms, and long-range scheduling are but a few of the assignments that must be undertaken from 24 to not less than 12 months in advance of an opening date.

A vital pre-opening budgetary requirement and function is the funding and drafting of furniture, fixtures, and equipment (FF&E) specifications. For major facilities, the FF&E budget can run into millions of dollars depending upon what has or has not been included in the general contract and earlier bid awards. In an arena, for example, fixed and/or telescopic seating may or may not be a part of the overall construction contract. Carpeting and interior furnishings may or may not be included in a convention center package.

Assuming the task of writing equipment specifications is to be undertaken by private management, it should be recognized that due to its labor-intensive nature pre-opening work of this magnitude will be expensive. Contracts for services such as these provide for determination of the necessary equipment, writing of specifications, issuance of proper bid documents, receipt of bids, and award of contracts. Receipt, inspection, and acceptance of all items involved completes the process.

In most communities, special care must be taken in the drafting of specifications as well as their conveyance documents to ensure that all legal requirements in that particular jurisdiction are properly handled. To avoid delays, challenges, and any hint of impropriety, the experience and knowledge of the firm engaged to perform this service should be thoroughly investigated in advance. If the private firm selected for management is not properly qualified for this specific service, other arrangements must be pursued.

Whether certain pre-opening functions are considered part of the overall management contract or as special services for which extra compensation will be paid is usually a matter of negotiation and may well differ from one project to another. Regardless, during the months preceding an opening determination must be made regarding services to be outsourced and those to be handled in-house by full-time employees. In instances where it is determined that outside assistance is needed, management usually works with the municipality in selecting the contractor or contractors and negotiating terms. Often outside contractors are sought to provide parking, security, trash removal, ticketing, electrical and phone maintenance, and audiovisual services.

EVENT PRODUCTION AND PROMOTION

Obviously, some of the major reasons for selecting private over public management are hopes of greater rental income, an increase in food and beverage revenues, a broader menu of services, and improvement in user approval.

Depending upon the type of building involved as well as its geographic location, certain opportunities to boost occupancy are often more readily available to the private operator. It should be recognized, however, that possibilities for dramatic change are more prevalent in arenas than convention centers or any other type of facility. The basic reason is that arenas normally offer a broader potential base of usage than do convention centers, theaters, or stadiums.

An initial move by private management after assuming responsibility for a building is often to conduct an in-depth review of existing marketing programs to determine both cost and effectiveness. In some circumstances, representatives of the private management company may have an advantage due to their ongoing relationships with the firms or individuals responsible for booking and routing major attractions. Private operators are quick to point out that their national offices work closely with promoters in efforts to develop block, or even exclusive, schedules favoring facilities under their control. For promoters of touring attractions such arrangements can prove extremely timesaving in avoiding the necessity for negotiating rental terms, service fees, concession and novelty rights, and many other details with each building on the tour.

In addition to marketing facilities to known users, private operators also attempt to fill voids in the normal schedule of activity through creation of new events and partnerships or cosponsorships with promoters of untested productions. At least two of the major firms maintain departments dedicated to event production and promotion.

The element of risk is prevalent in such endeavors and it is here the private operator has a marked advantage over public management. When the management of a publicly operated facility becomes involved in either promotion or co-promotion, any losses, even though they may be limited to rental fees, must come from public funds unless some prior arrangement has been made for subsidization by a private group. To avoid such criticism, whether the venture is successful or not, private firms take great care to treat such activities in an arms-length manner by charging themselves the same rental fees and service charges as would be required for anyone.

While efforts to create new events for slack periods are commendable, such activities must be carefully analyzed if private management is to avoid the charge by local and regional promoters that what they perceive as unfair competition erodes their business opportunities. It becomes even more difficult to defend in-house promotions in smaller communities where consumer events such as the auto show or home show may be sponsored by local associations representing those businesses.

FOOD AND BEVERAGE

Expansion and exploitation of food and beverage opportunities in the past decade have proven more dramatic than any other aspect insofar as the economics of public assembly facility design and management are concerned. Concession outlets in playhouses and theaters remain extremely limited for a variety of reasons, but for convention centers, arenas, and stadiums the gastronomical choices now range from the traditional hot dog to a seven-course candlelit dinner.

Part of the reason historically for delayed recognition of the potential profits from food and beverage operations was the attitude of those responsible for design and operation. Owners and operators of private baseball parks were, for the most part, more concerned with their teams, field conditions, and other matters than with food outlets. While profitable, concessions were still just part of the package and necessary to keep the fans happy. In retrospect, the national economy and the lack of expendable dollars at that time may have played a role in those early management decisions.

Concession stands were usually tucked under the seating forms or risers with little regard to their convenience or attractiveness, utilities or other matters. Some studies were available to indicate what was believed to be the desired running footage of counter space to adequately serve the public, but even this vital statistic was not a priority. Hawkers vending their wares through the stands were expected to close the gap in supply versus demand. There was a consensus that stands would sell more product if placed near restrooms. Concession menus were largely limited to popcorn, hot dogs, soft drinks, and beer. Even under such conditions, it was a highly lucrative business, with operators bragging about the profits of selling "paper and ice," meaning a paper cup loaded with ice and a minimum of soft drink.

Gradually, concession operators and arena management

awakened to the fact that additional items could be introduced without impacting the sale of old favorites. This, of course, led to the need for additional sales outlets, many of which were necessarily portable in nature. As newer arenas and stadiums were envisioned, more and more attention was paid to providing adequate and appealing space for both concession and novelty outlets.

Covered stadiums such as the Astrodome in Houston and the Superdome in New Orleans, with their executive suites and private dining rooms, proved to be a breakthrough in developing appropriate schematics for new stadiums and arenas. Today, almost all arenas and stadiums serving major league basketball, football, baseball, and hockey teams feature extensive levels of service. Catered food and beverage service is available in most executive skyboxes. Private dining rooms restricted to season ticket holders or other VIPs offer top quality food and service. In many cities public dining rooms with broad menus are open for all home games.

For fans unable to avail themselves of upper-level service, modern design now provides, in some instances, for food courts offering more circulation space and the availability of brand-name products such as McDonald's and Taco Bell in addition to the traditional items offered by the in-house concessionaire.

Convention centers experienced a somewhat different history as local authorities fretted over how to provide first-class food and beverage service for lessees in spite of complaints from local hotel operators that the governmentally operated venue represented unfair competition. A second problem was that of designing exhibition halls so that permanent concession stands would not interfere with differing exhibit booth layouts. Some efforts were made to include full-time restaurants in facilities but for most of them it proved a financial and logistical struggle due to uncertain schedules of operation.

Credit for the gradual change in attitude probably should be given to the professional meeting planners and their unwavering demands that first-class quality food and service must be made available to their delegates. The concept of catering luncheons and banquets by off-site providers proved unacceptable almost everywhere. This led to the design and equipping of larger, full-scale, production kitchens capable of preparing dinners in-house for groups of virtually any reasonable size. The design of some centers have been such that food and beverage service can be made available to the general public when convention groups are not on hand.

Along with this new and greater production capability has come both the need and opportunity for the food and beverage operators in a convention center to promote and sell their product to local companies, groups, and the general public. This is unwelcome competition for hoteliers, but most have accepted the fact in view of overall market demands.

Under incentive agreements in most management contracts, the private firm is in a better position to plan and finance aggressive sales and marketing campaigns designed to increase food and beverage revenues. In some situations, the private operator may also be able to accept a risk position in providing optional food choices such as a cafeteria for delegates. Some are offering food and beverage deliveries direct to booths during shows when exhibitors are unable or unwilling to take time away from their displays. As with arenas and stadiums, designers of convention centers now favor inclusion of food courts with brand-name outlets where appropriate. New products and the opportunities for portability are expanding possibilities even more.

With a broader base from which to evaluate food and beverage revenues for various events, the private management firm has an advantage over public administrators who may, or may not, be able to avail themselves of necessary data from similar facilities. In most instances where proposals are requested for exclusive concessions rights in a venue, decisions in the public sector must be based for the most part on which firm bids the highest percentage of gross receipts. Often, however, this may not be a true picture of the best long-term results for a facility if, in fact, a firm offering a slightly lower percentage can consistently produce sufficiently higher overall gross figures to offset the difference.

In most instances, contracts are awarded to concessionaires

and/or food and beverage firms for a stipulated period of time, with given rates for the percentages to be paid, and with appropriate protection for the facility ownership regarding prices, quality, and public liability. In some instances, separate contracts are awarded for concessions and for catering or food and beverage rights.

In retrospect, the opportunity to meet the ever-growing gastronomical requirements of the public may well be one of the primary keys to the success of privatization. Unfettered by the need to sidestep conflict with or criticism from the private sector, management firms have moved boldly into the sector of operations which yields the greatest profits. With Ogden Corporation as the primary owner of Ogden Entertainment and Aramark (ARA Services) as a principal stockholder in Spectacor there can be little question that companies of stature recognize the potential offered by almost every form of public assembly event.

CUSTODIAL AND MAINTENANCE SERVICES

Under conditions where the city, county, or state is intent upon operating a facility with the minimum possible permanent staff, responsibility for custodial services, building maintenance, engineering, and similar functions is often contracted to private companies. Transferral of these activities from the public sector is intended to result in a smaller number of public employees, realignment of job assignments, use of more part-time or temporary help, and possible renegotiation of certain union agreements. Custodial or maintenance contracts may include incentive clauses to reward the private operator for overall savings in operational costs.

The custodial work required in an assembly building, unlike many public facilities, will vary dramatically according to the scope and attendance at any given event. As a result, a flexible program for the scheduling of cleanup personnel becomes a virtual necessity and implementation of such a system is sometimes difficult under more rigid public employment requirements. In many instances, a stablized corps of custodial workers is employed for daily cleaning of areas in regular use with casual labor scheduled as needed to meet heavy demands.

PROMOTION AND MARKETING

Promotion and marketing activities take on many forms in today's world, with both emphasis and opportunity dependent to a great degree on the type of facility, its geographic location, and demographics. While there is usually little that can be done to substantially alter theater and playhouse occupancy, the possibilities are far greater in both convention centers and arenas, due primarily to the broader range of events which can be accommodated.

Reported convention center expenditures for promotion and advertising reveal annual budget figures ranging from zero to more than a million dollars in one rare instance (Mee 1994). Examination of this single budget item in respect to its effectiveness, plus a comparison of expenditures by competitors, could in itself aid in determining whether or not the sum is reasonable. Evaluation of a marketing and promotion budget could be carried out by public management, but private companies have the advantage of readily reviewing the budget figures of other facilities under their control, assessing results, and then advising the monitoring agency that a reduction in costs might be prudent.

Insofar as individual events are concerned, at least one of the major firms requires its staff to prepare a comprehensive marketing plan prior to all major functions. An analysis and recap of actual results is conducted after the event. Following review by the local marketing staff, the information is then forwarded to corporate offices, which distributes the data to other facilities that may be scheduled to present the same event, or a similar event, soon. A practice such as this limits mistakes and provides suggestions for improving strategies in the future.

Still another area in which multi-facility private firms hold some degree of advantage over public operations is in the field of customized event sponsorships which may be targeted toward specific consumer markets on behalf of corporations. In today's more sophisticated world of advertising and promotion, many companies are seeking ways to interact with their consumers via sports and entertainment events. Even more demanding is the fact that many of these firms are interested in such sponsorships *only* when they can be conducted in a particular marketplace.

It is here that the specialized departments of the private operator can prove most effective in identifying potential corporate clients, coupling this data with accurate demographic information regarding communities in which their facilities are located, and then seeking the type of event which can prove beneficial to all concerned. A good example of this where arenas are concerned are tennis tournaments. If a corporation concludes that a substantial segment of its existing or potential customers are tennis fans, the firm can then be expected to contribute sponsorship dollars in exchange for heavy promotion and wide exposure. The fact that the private management company is able to guarantee the facility against any losses rapidly brings any such venture into the realm of possibility, and especially so if the event is a newcomer in a test market.

Chapter 9

THE CONTRACT

One of the more critical factors in ensuring a healthy and pleasant relationship between a public body and a private management company is a well-written and mutually understood contract for services. Regardless of whether the agreement is for a new building or one which has been under public management, the document must clearly reflect both realistic goals and parameters of responsibility.

A review of many private management contracts indicates that certain items are common to all.

- Facility name
- Location
- Size description
- Name of owner
- Type of location
- Detailed identification of all concerned parties
- Length of initial term
- Renewal options
- Base management fee
- Incentive fee
- Caveats and exceptions

No contract should be considered proper without the customary paragraphs of legal language which set forth the background of the project, definitions, scope of services, specific services, booking (or scheduling) procedures, insurance, liability, indemnification, right of entry, appropriate accounting records and procedures, annual audits, periodic reporting, compliance with or ownership of certain permits, licenses, and taxes, termination procedures, force majeure, and identification of the individuals to whom all official notices or other communications shall be addressed.

Especially during shifts from public to private management, contracts should stipulate all existing prior agreements or commitments, identify agreed-upon objectives, and provide a reasonable length of time for their attainment. Civic officials in some situations have sought private management to improve occupancy, reduce operating costs, or improve user satisfaction. In still other cities there has been the need for renegotiation of contracts with subcontractors, concessionaires, and/or unions by someone other than an elected official or public employee. In most cases contracts for overall private management of a facility are in the range of three to five years. Where legally permissible, private firms often seek to include benchmarks wherein extension of the agreement will take effect automatically when certain predetermined goals are achieved.

Obviously, the base management fee will vary depending not only upon the size and complexity of the facility but to some extent on the geographic location of the venue as well. Generally speaking, fees for operating some arenas and convention centers in the mid-1990s were well in excess of $300,000 annually. Management fees for smaller properties such as theaters or trade centers ranged as low as $60,000. For many reasons, not the least of which is that almost all such contracts are public documents, there can be little question that specific definition of what is to be included in the base fee is of extreme importance.

Almost without exception, the base figure includes not only day-to-day operation of the facility or facilities, but also corporate support, oversight, and recommendations. Depending upon the capabilities of the operator, the fee could also cover food and beverage services, marketing and sales, ticket distribution, security and crowd management, parking, and a score of other assignments.

Early in the history of private management, the salary and benefits of the general manager or facility director were included in the base management fee. Some of the logic behind this was to enable a management firm to pay whatever salary was believed necessary to attract the right person for the job. Secondly, it served to shield on-site management from personal criticism by the media or city department heads if the manager's salary proved substantially above local standards. This factor proved not as sensitive as first believed; many contracts are now treating all salaries and operating expenses as pass-through budget items.

In addition to establishing the base management fee, most contracts include a series of incentive clauses. These may reflect targets or milestones for improvement in revenues, occupancy, attendance, or perhaps reduction of operational expenses. For example, if a facility has demonstrated an average operating loss of say $1 million annually, the management firm might receive a bonus or incentive of some mutually agreed-upon percentage (ranging from 20% or higher) of any reduction in that figure. The bonus or incentive figure may, in some cases, be balanced against a percentage of the base fee. Here again, it is vital that the contract be specific in detailing how incentive figures are to be computed.

Virtually all agreements stipulate that the private operator must prepare and submit an annual operating budget to be approved by the appropriate jurisdiction. While arrangements are usually made for appropriate reviews and possible adjustments in budget figures to fit changing conditions, at the same time the operator must be assured that necessary funds for proper operation of the facility will be made available. If not, contract terms should provide the private operator the opportunity to terminate the relationship and be appropriately compensated for any corporate losses in doing so. The contract must also set forth details of when the private management firm may bill for its contract services and the period of time for receipt of payment. In some instances it is acceptable for the operator to draw payment of the management fee from the operating revenue account once annually; in other situations it may be paid on a quarterly or monthly basis.

In the case of facilities which have been under public management there have been situations where, in order for private management to be implemented, it has been necessary to accept and maintain the status quo regarding certain employees, interdepartmental practices, or perhaps labor agreements. As delicate and potentially embarassing as these situations may be, an understanding by all parties concerned of how they are to be handled must be reflected in final contract terms.

When negotiations between municipalities and private management representatives extend over long periods of time, occasional progress reports to facility employees are helpful. Reassurance should be given the work force that their interests are of primary concern and that, should a management change be implemented, ample time will be provided for personal decisions. Updates serve both to dispel unfounded rumors and, of even greater importance, help sustain staff morale during such interim periods.

As most public assembly facilities are governmentally owned, the issuance of periodic progress reports for public consumption can be helpful in gaining acceptance and support. Most of the major firms not only prepare such statements but also schedule regular meetings with key civic administrators to review current operations and future action plans as well. To further good relations between owner and operator, many jurisdictions appoint a contract monitor whose specific duty is to serve as liaison with the private management firm.

Chapter 10

THE COMPANIES

While the concept of private management for individual public assembly structures is far from new, only in the past decade has the industry witnessed the creation of corporations designed to undertake operation of multiple facilities scattered throughout the United States and overseas.

Madison Square Garden Corporation (MSG) is considered the oldest private management company of an arena facility. Formed more than 100 years ago, MSG manages the New York City sports arena, a privately owned facility. Owner of the New York Rangers of the National Hockey League and the New York Knickerbockers of the National Basketball Association, MSG is said to have evolved from a publicly traded New York Stock Exchange company to a closely held subsidiary of Paramount Communications.

As early as the 1950s, some National Hockey League owners were managing facilities—primarily ice arenas and some publicly owned—where they operated minor league teams. One example was Arthur Wirtz, owner of the Chicago Black Hawks, whose organization oversaw the Indiana State Fairgrounds Coliseum in Indianapolis. Understandably, interest in those days focused on the league schedule, practice times, welfare of the hockey team, and little else. Few, if any, of the owners expanded their interests beyond one operation; facility management per se was of secondary importance.

The Houston Sports Association, Inc. (HSA) was among the first companies to manage a publicly owned facility. The Association was formed in the early 1960s primarily to acquire a ma-

jor league baseball team for Houston. Upon award of a franchise, HSA then negotiated with county officials to build and
operate the now world-renowned Houston Astrodome. Similar
to many of the arrangements in cities where the team owner's
company operates the property in which the team plays, the
Houston group since its inception has focused its attention
strongly on operation of the Astrodome and its exposition-ori-
ented neighbor the Astrohall.

Another movement toward private management came with
the leaseback of the Omni arena from the City of Atlanta, Georgia, to Tom Cousins, owner of the primary tenant-to-be Atlanta
Hawks of the National Basketball League. Here again, the primary interest of civic leaders was to provide financial incentive
for the investors and a home for the new professional team.

Close to, but not entirely outside the realm of the public sector, another version of the leaseback concept was the Oakland-
Alameda County Coliseum Complex in Oakland, California,
constructed and operated by a quasi-public group headed by
Edgar Kaiser of World War II shipbuilding fame. The agreement
provided for both the City of Oakland and County of Alameda
to make annual contributions sufficient to subsidize capital
costs and then enter into a contract permitting the facility build-
ers to manage the complex. The basic purpose and result was to
provide homes for major league baseball, football, and basketball teams.

In Indianapolis, Indiana, a nine-man partnership known
as Market Square Associates developed a leaseback agreement
with the City of Indianapolis for Market Square Arena. The
building was constructed to serve as home court for the Indiana
Pacers of the then-American Basketball Association (ABA),
which later became a part of the National Basketball Association (NBA). The long-term lease enabled the Associates to purchase a hockey team, the Indiana Racers, and to provide not only
management but promotional activities for the facility as well.
Denzil E. Skinner, who had previously served as the general manager of the Charleston, West Virginia, Civic Center and the Norfolk Scope in Norfolk, Virginia, turned from public to private
management by becoming Managing Partner for the Associates.

The birthplace of multiple private management as practiced

today in the United States—beyond the scope of a single facility—is believed to have been a luncheon following ground-
breaking ceremonies for the New Orleans Hyatt Regency Hotel,
which is located contiguous to the Superdome. It was here that
Edwin Edwards, Governor of Louisiana at that time, suggested
to A. N. Pritzker, owner of Hyatt Hotels, that "since you people
manage hotels, hospitals and numerous other businesses, why
don't you consider running the Superdome. Having a busy,
well-run Superdome surely must be important to your new hotel next door." The seed was planted and before returning to his
Chicago office, Pritzker promised the governor he would "see if
there is any way we can help" (Skinner 1995).

As the nation's second covered stadium (after the Astrodome
in Houston), the Louisiana Superdome had opened in 1975 to
great acclaim. It was then, and is still, ranked as one of the won-
ders of the world. Initially programmed to serve not only sports
but large conventions as well, the New Orleans project encoun-
tered financial problems from the outset. Political patronage,
unprofessional operation, and a myriad of sweetheart labor contracts all helped to create operating losses reportedly in the
range of six million dollars annually. Understandably, Louisiana
state officials were seeking ways to unload or at least control
this politically embarrassing situation.

Prior to this time, Pritzker had been briefly exposed to private
management of a publicly owned facility in Rosemont, Illinois,
(near Chicago's O'Hare Field) where the Hyatt company for a
short period of time operated a small exhibition hall which had
been built by the city as an enhancement to attract a Hyatt Hotel
to the community. The agreement, however, lasted only briefly
due to conflicts and complaints from competing hoteliers.

In response to the suggestion from Governor Edwards,
Pritzker contacted a friend and business associate, Fred "Bud"
Tucker, owner of the Indianapolis Hyatt Hotel and Chairman of
Market Square Associates, who in turn suggested that Pritzker
call Skinner to determine if he would be willing to devote some
time to consult on the problem. After a few trips to New Orleans
and countless talks with Pritzker, Skinner was on his way to
Louisiana. The launching of Facility Management, Incorporated (FMI) in 1977 was the end result.

Unlike today, when attorneys can explore and use existing private management contracts from other cities as prototypes, the Superdome document was a first. Fortunately, Skinner was aided by a willing, and even anxious, governor and attorney general who assisted in developing a contract that would allow the Pritzker group to be successful and, at the same time, permit the Louisiana state government to walk away from most of the problem.

In contrast to many current contracts, there was a degree of financial risk for the new Superdome management company. The agreement did, however, specify an incentive figure wherein FMI was to be compensated by a percentage of the amount which operational costs could be reduced. The figure was later criticized by some as overly generous, but it cannot be overlooked that at the time of signing there were no guarantees on either side that all, or any, of the reductions and cutbacks envisioned could be achieved.

It was understandable then that to the surprise of some and the joy of many, the first year of private operation of the Superdome resulted in a bottom line improvement of more than $4 million and a heartening reward for the new management company. (The total has been reported in the range of $1 million or more.) Skinner and his organization were deluged with more offers to take over other facilities than they had time to explore. It should also be mentioned that while Louisiana officials and FMI understood the need for cost-cutting moves, the procedures were not viewed with equal pleasure by many others, including unions and labor groups affected. Threats and scare tactics proved of little avail, however, and soon faded as the success of the move began receiving the plaudits of both local and national media.

Skinner was acclaimed by *Time* magazine as an industry pioneer and to him must go much of the credit for establishment of private management as it is known today. Building on his success in New Orleans, Skinner expanded the concept not only nationally but internationally as well.

In response to inquiries from throughout the United States regarding the possibility of taking over management of other public assembly facilities, FMI moved slowly and cautiously, with Skinner declining more opportunities than he accepted. In spite of the Louisiana success, from the beginning he cautioned that private management agreements were "generally the least desirable for the owner," but added that "with the proper contract there are literally dozens of cities where contract management could provide a genuine service" (Skinner 1995).

Under Skinner's leadership, FMI expanded its interests to include management of a wide variety of arenas and convention centers such as Moscone Convention Center in San Francisco, California; Nassau Veterans Memorial Coliseum in Uniondale, New York; Miami Beach Convention Center in Miami Beach, Florida; the Long Beach Convention and Entertainment Center in Long Beach, California; and many others. Discussions and negotiations with both existing and planned facilities were launched not only throughout North America but in Asia and Europe as well. As facilities were added, the parent Facility Management Incorporated became known more commonly as Facility Management Group (FMG) to reflect corporate legalities in various parts of the country.

SPECTACOR MANAGEMENT GROUP (SMG)

The demise of Facility Management Group as such came soon after the death of A. N. Pritzker, whose sons and heirs determined that the widespread interests of the family holdings should be reduced, or at least restructured. As a partner and shareholder in FMG, Skinner battled valiantly to purchase the corporation outright only to see it merged in 1988 with Spectacor Management Corporation of Philadelphia, a company privately held by Ed Snider and his family, whose holdings include the Philadelphia Flyers NHL hockey club and the CoreStates Spectrum which serves as home for the Flyers and the Philadelphia 76ers of the National Basketball Association. By virtue of the agreement, Skinner found himself legally barred for a period of years from organizing a competing company or from any type of consulting regarding contract management.

The sale or merger of FMG with Spectacor came as something of a surprise in the industry. Prior to that time, the Snider family had confined its interests to professional sports and contract management of the Philadelphia Spectrum, the Philadelphia Civic Center, and one regional client, the nearby Centrum in Worcester, Massachusetts. Renamed Spectacor Management Group (SMG), it rightfully claimed the title of "world's largest company specializing in private management of public assembly facilities."

Since 1988 after acquiring FMG which had some 15 or 16 sites under management and $23.4 million in revenues, SMG has expanded to 33 or more contracts covering 57 distinct building operations which range from a 2,000-seat theater in Mobile, Alabama, to the 76,000-seat Superdome. Market share for SMG in the field is preeminent at 47%, with the company operating twice as many facilities as its leading competitor.

Initially, SMG was a closely held joint venture with ownership attributed to Spectacor (the Snider family); Pritzker Family Interests; and ARA Services, Inc. (ARAMARK), a multibillion dollar company specializing in food services and institutional feeding. On January 5, 1998, Spectacor sold its share of the ownership to the other partners under an arrangement in the original partnership agreement which provided that should one partner make an offer to buy which was rejected, the remaining partners could match that offer and purchase the firm for themselves. Similar to the situation with Skinner, Snider is now barred from establishing a private management firm for a specified number of years, according to *Amusement Business* (January 12, 1998).

Company promotional material states SMG is "unparalled in the field of private facility management due to our ownership structure and some 50-plus dedicated corporate support personnel." Illustrating the posture of management firms that a major benefit offered by them is efficient business management as contrasted to hands-on facility management is that the current president of Spectacor Management was not recruited from the ranks of the public assembly facility industry.

In addition to management SMG has developed other divisions to provide specialized services. For example, it is the responsibility of SMG Productions division to produce, package, manage, and market events at facilities operated by SMG. These include sporting events, family entertainment, holiday and seasonal spectaculars, concerts, cultural presentations, and extravaganzas.

Still another division is SMG Sports, which is charged with the production of additional sports activities at SMG-affiliated buildings. A third division is Network International which develops advertising, merchandising, entertainment and vending concepts for companies that use sports and entertainment to reach their target markets. Recently, SMG created a convention center division, whose objectives are to provide corporate sales, marketing and promotional support for those venues. Similar to its competition, SMG offers a full range of consulting or developmental services to assist during the planning, construction, expansion and renovation of facilities.

Even though strong interest has been shown by all the private management companies in expanding into international markets, incursion into Europe or Asia has been slow indeed. The SMG company profile lists Sheffield Arena in Sheffield, England, as one of its overseas accounts and adds that consulting services are being provided the Oslo Spektrum in Oslo, Norway.

Although business relationships are constantly subject to change, the following is a partial list of major facilities reported to be under Spectacor management:

Atlantic City Convention Hall, Atlantic City, NJ
Broward County Convention Center, Ft. Lauderdale, FL
Centrum Arena, Worcester, MA
Colorado Convention Complex, Denver, CO
Cook Convention Center, Memphis, TN
CoreStates Center, Philadelphia, PA
CoreStates Spectrum, Philadelphia, PA
Grand Center, Van Andel Arena, Grand Rapids, MI
Honolulu Convention Center, Honolulu, HI
Kansas Expocenter, Topeka, KS
Knickerbocker Arena, Albany, NY
Long Beach Convention Center, Long Beach, CA
Los Angeles Memorial Coliseum, Los Angeles, CA
Louisiana Superdome, New Orleans, LA
Miami Beach Convention Center, Miami Beach, FL

Mobile Convention Center and Exhibition Hall, Mobile, AL
Moscone Center, Civic Auditorium & Brooks Hall, San Francisco, CA
Nassau Veterans Memorial Coliseum, Long Island, NY
Niagara Falls Civic Facilities, Niagara Falls, NY
Peoria Civic Facilities, Peoria, IL
Osborn Convention Center, Jacksonville, FL
Rhode Island Convention Center, Providence, RI
Richmond Coliseum, Richmond, VA
Riverside Complex, Baton Rouge, LA
Salt Palace Convention Center, Salt Lake City, UT
Three Rivers Stadium, Pittsburgh, PA
Soldier Field, Chicago, IL

OGDEN ENTERTAINMENT SERVICES (OES)

Second to SMG in the number of facilities under contract is Ogden Entertainment Services, a division of Ogden Corporation. The parent company, publicly held with approximately $1.9 billion in revenues and some 42,000 employees, specializes in aviation, property management, waste-to-energy operations, and a variety of industrial and technological services to the governmental and public sectors. Unlike those whose focus is confined to facility management, Ogden could almost be considered a veritable "department store" of facility services.

Long prominent as a concessions and catering operator, Ogden Corporation was a familiar name in the industry for many years prior to moving into facility management. Ogden made its entry into this phase of the business in 1982 by acquiring the little-known Alpine-Butco company, which had two accounts, the Sullivan Arena and the Egan Convention Center, both in Anchorage, Alaska.

Three years later in 1985, Ogden was the successful bidder to provide management services for the Jacob Javits Convention Center in New York City. Later that year, Ogden added Pensacola Civic Center in Pensacola, Florida, and the El Centro Convention Center in El Centro, California, to its client roster. Shortly after, Ogden Executive Vice President John MacAniff in

1986 named Douglas Logan, then general manager of the Rockford Civic Center in Rockford, Illinois, to manage Ogden's new Facility Management Division.

Responsive to growth, the division's name was changed to Ogden Entertainment in 1991 to "better reflect broad based services provided to sports, entertainment and leisure venues." Logan departed Ogden Entertainment in 1994 to form OCESA Presents in Mexico City and in 1995, Loris Smith rejoined the firm as Senior Vice President of Ogden Entertainment. Smith had previously worked for Ogden as executive director of Javits but had moved from that post to serve a brief period of time as Executive Vice President of TicketMaster. Smith retired from Ogden in 1997.

Although Ogden is gaining stature in management activities, food and beverage operations remain the company's strong suit and the most lucrative. The firm reportedly has management contracts for some 17 facilities nationally, including arenas such as Target Center in Minneapolis, Minnesota, and Great Western Forum in Inglewood, California. Corporate information stipulates Ogden "manages 51 venues at 37 locations around the world. International accounts include facilities in Canada, Mexico, England, Germany, Australia, Thailand, and Argentina."

Ogden made its initial appearance on the international scene by assuming control of the Palacio de los Deportes in Mexico City. Corporate headquarters advises the Entertainment group has opened two arenas recently in the United Kingdom, one of which is the largest modern indoor entertainment center in Europe, the Manchester Arena.

In addition to its food and beverage operations, Ogden provides specialized services including event booking, security, parking, ticketing, and janitorial at more than 90 stadiums, arenas, racetracks, and parks throughout America. The firm also offers financial feasibility studies and technical expertise during the design, construction, and pre-opening of new buildings.

Although subject to change, a partial list of facilities managed by Ogden Entertainment Services includes:

Arrowhead Pond, Anaheim, CA
Brisbane Entertainment Centre, Brisbane, Australia

Carlson Civic Center, Fairbanks, AK
Edmonton Coliseum, Edmonton, AB
Egan Convention Center, Anchorage, AL
Fargodome, Fargo, ND
Five Seasons Center, Cedar Rapids, IA
Great Western Forum, Los Angeles, CA
Hartford Civic Center, Hartford, CN
Meadowlands Convention Center, Seacaucus, NJ
Hilton Coliseum & Stephens Auditorium, Ames, IA
Pershing Auditorium, Lincoln, NE
Pensacola Civic Center, Pensacola, FL
Providence Civic Center, Providence, R.I.
Rosemont Horizon, Rosemont, IL
Bayfront Auditorium & Saenger Theater, Pensacola, FL
Sioux Falls Arena and Convention Center, Sioux Falls, IA
Southern Star Amphitheater, Tinley Park, IL
Sullivan Arena, Anchorage, AK
Target Arena, Minneapolis, MN
Wallace Civic Center, Fitchburg, MS

LEISURE MANAGEMENT
INTERNATIONAL (LMI)

The origin of Leisure Management International (LMI), currently the third largest private management company in America, began in the summer of 1984 when Mike McGee, present Chairman of the LMI Board, and Neal Gunn, then Vice President of the Astrodome, agreed to be part of a team pursuing the rights to develop, construct, and manage a facility that was being considered by the Miami Sports and Exhibition Authority on behalf of the city of Miami. In the fall of 1984, Facility Management and Marketing (FM&M) was formed.

FM&M, as it was known then, was a 50/50 joint venture between an entity owned and totally controlled by John J. McMullen and another owned equally by Fidelity Mutual Life Insurance, Northwestern Mutual Life Insurance, Kenneth Schnitzer, and McGee. FM&M then aligned itself with two other partners both of Houston, Texas, to form Decoma Venture, a project-specific entity which was chosen to develop, construct, and manage the Miami Arena. This selection process took place in March of 1985. During the late summer of 1986, FM&M changed its name to Leisure Management International (LMI).

Some two and a half years after formation of Leisure Management International, Clifford B. Wallace, at that time general manager of the New Orleans Superdome, became a new player in the movement when he was hired by McGee to serve as president of LMI. Several years previously Skinner, needing more time to pursue national expansion of FMG, had selected Wallace, then manager of the Von Braun Civic Center in Huntsville, Alabama, to take over day-to-day operations.

The LMI partnership was reorganized in 1989 when McMullen acquired the interests held by Northwestern Mutual Life Insurance, Kenneth Schnitzer, and Fidelity Mutual Life Insurance to create a partnership between himself and McGee. This partnership remained intact until shortly after McMullen announced his intention to liquidate his sports and entertainment holdings in the Houston Astros and Houston Sports Association, then owners of the Astrodome and holders of the Astrodome lease and LMI. After lengthy negotiations, an investor group headed by McGee acquired 100% of LMI assets effective July 30, 1993. McGee became Board Chairman and General Partner; he then named John Blaisdell as President and Chief Operating Officer. Wallace accepted a lessor role in the new organization but left soon afterwards.

In the late summer of 1994, fifty percent of LMI was sold to H. Wayne Huizenga, founder of Waste Management, former Chairman of Blockbuster Video, former Vice Chairman of Viacom Communications and Chairman of Republic Industries. In addition, Huizenga at the present time owns the Miami Dolphins of the National Football League, the Florida Marlins of Major League Baseball and the Florida Panthers of the National Hockey League. Owners of Leisure Management International are Huizenga and a Houston Partnership Group of which McGee is a general partner.

Even though the time span cannot be considered great, details regarding the background and evolution of contract management as it exists today are already dependent upon personal recollections, viewpoints, or interpretations of facts. While many observers consider Facility Management Group the groundbreaker because it was the first to expand its operations from a single to multiple venues, McGee and his partners are firm in their opinion that FMG was not first in the contract management business. They contend that Leisure Management International was formed by principals of the Houston Sports Association, a private management company that had been in place since 1965, some 12 years prior to the formation of Facility Management Group.

The Houston Astrodome remains under the management of HSA. Again, while subject to change, the list of major LMI accounts includes:

Gwinnett Civic and Cultural Center, Duluth, GA
Knight International Center, Miami, FL
Monroe Civic Center, Monroe, LA
Palm Springs Convention Center, Palm Springs, CA
Ponchartrain Center, Kenner, LA
Pyramid, Memphis, TN
Nashville Arena, Nashville, TN
Miami Arena, Miami, FL
Pro Player Stadium, Miami, FL
Space Coast Stadium, Melbourne, FL
Summit, Houston, TX

GLOBE FACILITY SERVICES (GFS)

Running fourth in operational responsibilities is Globe Facility Services (GFS), a relative newcomer to the field, which currently lists an assortment of nine widely scattered properties under its supervision. Globe was organized in early 1994 by its three principals, Nicholas Flaskay, Chairman; Michel F. Sauers, President and Chief Operating Officer; and Kenneth J. Young, Director.

Highly experienced in the hospitality and entertainment industries, Flaskay also heads Globe Information Systems, a large scale computerized ticketing system in the United States. In addition to his responsibilities with GFS, Young serves as Executive Vice President for New Vista Services, a company which provides food and beverage services to a number of major venues.

Prior to joining GFS, Sauers held the position of Senior Vice President in charge of sales and marketing for Spectacor Management Group from 1986 to 1994. He began his career with SMG when it was founded in 1982 as one of the company's three corporate employees.

Based in Tampa, Florida, Globe has focused strong attention on the Asian market with a client list that includes the Putra World Trade Center and the Palace of Golden Horses in Kuala Lumpur, Malaysia, and the Bangkok International Exhibition Centre in Bangkok, Thailand. Other clients include the World Arena in Colorado Springs, Colorado; West Palm Beach Auditorium in West Palm Beach, Florida; Ohio State University in Columbus, Ohio; Harborview Center in Clearwater, Florida; Thomas H. White Stadium in Port St. Lucie, Florida; and the Deuteron Entertainment Center in Tampa, Florida.

CENTRE MANAGEMENT

Still another firm is Centre Management, which currently lists four east coast arenas under its supervision. This organization was formed in 1984 by Abe Pollin and Jerry Sacks of the Centre Group, owners of the Washington Capitals and Washington Bullets sports franchises and Capital Centre in Landover, Maryland.

In addition to Capital Centre, the client list includes Springfield, (Massachusetts) Civic Center and Baltimore (Maryland) Arena. In 1986, acquisition of the Patriot Center at George Mason University in Fairfax, Virginia, marked the first time a university had selected a private firm to manage its sports facility. The concept of privatization has evidently not proven of great interest to universities throughout the United States, with only a few following the lead of GMU.

THE OTHERS

Because a limited number of properties are eligible for privatization and all of them have been contacted many times over, strong competition exists among the major companies. Growth, or even maintenance of the status quo, has been difficult for smaller operators such as Olympia Arenas, Inc., of Detroit, Michigan, and Russ Cline and Associates of St. Petersburg, Florida.

Two additional management firms which should be mentioned are the Nederlander Organization and Pace Entertainment Group. Both are large organizations and major players in the industry but to date have confined their interests primarily to large-scale outdoor theaters and pavilions, some of which are publicly owned.

Since facility representatives seeking management proposals are understandably influenced by the experience and recommendations of other communities, it is difficult for a start-up company to gain a foothold in the industry. Some have established a regional presence but found little success in expanding nationally. If this domination of the market will encourage major firms to increase their management fees to the point where private management will become economically unattractive remains to be seen. Simultaneously, the major firms must determine if adequate profit margins can be derived at any price by providing corporate oversight to smaller venues in less accessible locations.

Chapter 11

THE TRANSITION PROCESS

Not unlike reorganization or downsizing in the corporate world, transition from public to private management of an assembly facility can generate a broad variety of reactions and emotions. Lessees may find their situations altered to some degree; suppliers may face heightened demands for service; the lives and/or careers of many employees may be changed. There is little chance that transition will prove painless for everyone.

Both good and bad transitions have been noted, but the interests of all seem best served when management has moved slowly in implementation of necessary changes and when employees have been encouraged to offer their recommendations for improving operations in which they are involved. Usually the majority of staff members who wish to stay are retained. Every effort should be made by private management to alleviate employee anxiety through periodic written updates, staff meetings, or personal contact.

When assuming control of a property which has been on-line for many years, most private operators have developed set procedures designed to minimize the impact of the transition. Obviously, the program must be modified for each location, with the speed of action dependent upon the severity of local conditions. In some instances, a transition team comprised of corporate representatives with a variety of special talents has been temporarily assigned to provide assistance to the general manager.

Ideally, employment of an experienced manager with transition experience from another city would appear to be of great benefit in dealing with a newly privatized venue. Otherwise, the choice would probably be a veteran operator possessing a strong resume from a similar building. If, however, the individual chosen as general manager lacks what might be considered appropriate credentials, initial assistance where required is provided from corporate headquarters.

Early transition responsibilities for both the management company and its general manager include the review of the following: all contracts for use of the facility; rental rates and service fees; contracts for services such as catering, concessions, and security; union contracts; long-term scheduling commitments; and other related documents. Meetings with primary tenants are conducted, and systems are established to keep civic officials apprised of all activities.

Concurrent with other activities, the management company institutes an evaluation of all employees. Other tasks include a review and update of job descriptions and possibly the establishment of a new Table of Organization for the facility. Employees should also anticipate an in-depth examination of their benefits and the possible development of alternate plans.

It is not uncommon for a management firm to be requested to honor long-standing agreements of one nature or another, sometimes political. For example, when civil service is to be eliminated from a facility, a common practice has been to permit those who wish to stay within the system to transfer to some other department of the city, county, or state government. In rare instances where this option has proved a hardship, the individual has been allowed to retain employment at the facility but with special considerations.

Although it may be in the best interests of all concerned to retain and retrain the majority of facility employees, the management firm can be expected to employ its own personnel in those positions considered most critical to the stability and success of the venture. In addition to the director or general manager, the positions that can be expected to be filled by corporate representatives are usually those of operations director, marketing director, and finance director. This practice not only provides individuals well versed in corporate policy, but also serves

as a training ground for those destined for greater future responsibilities.

Looking in general at transition from public to private management it is impossible to establish an across-the-board time-
table applicable to every situation. Many aspects of the procedure can be completed within a few months, but some changes
simply must be deferred until the appropriate moment.

Chapter 12

THE FUTURE
OF PRIVATIZATION

Even though it has become an accepted and successful option for some, contract management cannot at this point be considered an industry trend; nor will it ever become the universal answer for all management situations.

Private management company officials confidently and understandably predict a steady growth for the concept. Nevertheless, the increase in privatization is expected to slow as time goes on simply because the market is limited: first by the number of facilities for which the plan may be appropriate, and second by the number of facilities in which management firms themselves are interested. An additional factor is the nature of the public assembly facility industry, which has been historically slow in the acceptance of change.

Whether or not privatization can be considered a *trend* may be somewhat like deciding if a cup is half-full or half-empty. Statistical information from the Industry Profile Study (IPS) conducted by the International Association of Assembly Managers indicated that only 13% of all publicly owned facilities participating in the study are privately operated. From a listing of 113 arenas, 13.1% reported having private management; of 84 convention centers, 8.2% were privately managed; of 24 stadiums, 9.1% were under private guidance. Civic officials in most municipalities where facilities have been privatized say they are pleased with the results. The number of management contracts that have been extended for a period of years give further indication of satisfactory performance. Balancing these positive aspects is the research by Marc Ackerman which indicated "municipalities that have yet to fully investigate or pursue contract management remain skeptical regarding its eventual benefits and applicability to their unique situations" (Ackerman 1993).

Introduction of private management normally entails the loss of a measure of public authority or control. Politically, the concept of having no voice in hiring practices, rental rates, or scheduling priorities is not appealing, desirable, or perhaps acceptable in many communities.

Another adverse complication for communities considering a change to private management is the limited number of private operators from which to seek proposals. Competition is limited at the moment, leaving owners little opportunity to develop spirited bidding.

Looking beyond North America, acceptance of American-style privatization in both Europe and Asia can be expected to move at an even slower pace. The primary difference may well be one of definition since construction of some overseas buildings has been the result of private investors who, in turn, have had a voice in selecting the management system. London's Queen Elizabeth II Conference Centre is owned by the government, but in 1996 entered into a management contract with an in-house team headed by the Centre's managing director. Otherwise, Geoffrey Smith, editor of the Association Internationale des Palais de Congres' News writes, "My belief is that private management is unusual in Europe. Almost always the management is paid by the public authority, whatever sort this may be, that owns the facility" (Smith 1997).

In considering the most appropriate management system for any facility, operational costs, amount of annual subsidication required, occupancy, attendance, public acceptance, and lessee satisfaction are but a few of the critical factors to be evaluated. In brief, if public management is producing the best results that can be expected, why change? If there are rules or regulations applicable solely to public management which hinder efficient operation, would policy changes prove easier and less traumatic than turning to the private sector?

Establishment of a straightforward, plainly stated mission

statement is critical for the success of any facility. Unfortunately, when buildings are under the public administration, managers are often given few defined goals or objectives. Simplistic as it may sound, if there are no goals or objectives, what criteria can be used to measure the effectiveness of any form of management? To the credit of private management firms, they have learned that only by agreement on predetermined criteria such as acceptable operational deficits, occupancy, and community objectives can a management contract be binding and enforceable for either party.

Private operators must also be given due credit for recognizing that food and beverage merchandising is undoubtedly the most profitable operation in any facility whether it be an arena, stadium, or convention center. The focus on this area and the prominence of food operators as principals in the major management firms lend credibility to this observation.

In many situations, however, it cannot be overlooked that since the facilities were constructed with public funds to provide a special service or fill a community need, there are usually factors of equal, or greater importance, than that of finances which must be considered prior to abandonment of public management. In smaller communities an example could be the impact that adoption of contract management would have on the public image of the person assigned to manage that property. Instead of performing the role of a representative of the city or county and being expected to participate in local organizations such as the Jaycees, Lions Club, or Rotary Club, private sector managers would necessarily be corporate-oriented, rightfully owing their allegiance more to their firms than to the city in which they work.

Questions are endless; the answers are confusing. In his Heartland Policy Study, Professor Edwin Mills concluded, "Convention centers should be owned and *operated* by private firms." (Mills 1991) Mills, however, gives no hint as to why any private firm would, or should be, interested in owning a center. A similar question could be why do governments build stadiums and arenas from which *only* private operators (team owners) can profit?

If any conclusion regarding private versus public management can be reached, it is that adoption of a proper *administrative* plan can in the long run prove as important to the ultimate success or failure of a facility as choices concerning architectural or construction matters. Those responsible for selecting the system must of necessity familiarize themselves with the many advantages and disadvantages of the available options and then opt for the one offering the best solution for their community.

BIBLIOGRAPHY

Ackerman, A. M. (1993). *The trend toward privatization of public assembly facilities*. Unpublished master's thesis, Cornell University, Ithaca, New York.

Brady, E., & Howlett, D. (1996, September 6). Ballpark construction's booming. *USA Today*.

Deckard, L. (1998, January 12). Snider sells third of SMG to partners. *Amusement Business*.

Elliot, C. (1995). CVB-convention center mergers: Who'll be next? *Facilities, October*.

Herrick, J. (1996). Putting the pieces of the private management puzzle together. *Facility Manager, September*.

Hlestand, M. (1995, September 18). The biz: An inside look at the sports business. *USA Today*.

IAAM historical highlights. (1997). *IAAM Guide*.

IACVB convention income survey update. (1995). Conducted by Deloitte & Touche for the International Association of Convention and Visitor Bureaus Foundation.

Industry profile study. (1994). International Association of Assembly Managers.

Leisure Management, International company profile.

Mee, W. W. (1994). *Trends in convention center marketing*. Summary of an annual survey in cooperation with *Trade Show Week*; presented in October 1994.

Mills, E. S. (1991). *Should governments own convention centers?* Heartland Policy Study ISSN #0889-8014.

Ogden Entertainment Group company profile.

Petersen, D. (1996). *Sports, convention, and entertainment facilities*. Urban Land Institute. ULI Catalog No. S04.

———. (1992). Contract management: Why, how to do it. *Facility Manager, April*.

111

Powers, L. Convention-hall growth wisdom. *USA Today.*
Riley, J. (1996). Fields of green. *Arizona Republic, September.*
Skinner, D. E. (1995, November 12). (Personal communication; correspondence with author.)
Smith, G. V. (1997, July 24). Correspondence with author.
Spectacor Management Group company profile.
Tucson Convention Center operational assessment. (1995, February 14). Stein & Company, Chicago, IL.

SUGGESTED READING

Day, D. (1990). Privatization. *Facility Manager, Spring.*
———. (1990). Contract vs. inhouse. *Facility Manager, Summer.*
Engdahl, L. (1987). Pursuing private development: The Ganix game plan. *Facility Manager, Summer.*
Quinn, L. R. (1986). Privatization: Has its time come? *Facility Manager, Spring.*
Russo, F. (1992). Solutions through private management. *Facility Manager, April/June.*
Smith, J. K., McGee, M., & St. Clair, C. W. (1993). *Private/public management.* IAAM Foundation: Oglebay Monograph 101.
Twohig, K. (1992). *Facility management alternatives.* IAAM Foundation: Oglebay Monograph 201.
Williams, M. A. (1986). The benefits of going private. *Facility Manager, Spring.*

INDEX